INTRODUCTION

by Jeremy M. Norman

Among the most exotic and dramatic anatomical studies ever created, the striking series of anatomical plates reproduced in this book is attributed to Pietro Berrettini, usually called Pietro da Cortona (1596–1669) after his birthplace. Pietro was perhaps the most influential painter of the Italian Baroque movement, second only to Gian Lorenzo Bernini (1598–1680) in his overall achievement as a Roman High Baroque artist. He excelled as an architect, painter, decorator and designer of tombs and sculpture, although he was not a sculptor himself.

An almost exact contemporary of Bernini and Francesco Borromini (1599–1667), Pietro da Cortona was born at Cortona (near Arezzo in Tuscany) into a family of artisans. Most probably he received his first practical training in architecture by studying under his father, a stonemason. Later he was apprenticed to the undistinguished Florentine painter Andrea Commodi, whom he accompanied to Rome in 1612 or 1613. When Commodi returned to Florence in 1614, Pietro moved over to the studio of the equally unimpressive Florentine painter Baccio Ciarpi. He studied Raphael and the antique with great devotion during these years of uninspiring apprenticeship. While most seventeenth-century artists immersed themselves in these subjects, it was particularly significant in Pietro's case, since he could not learn much from his teachers. In fact, it was Pietro's devotion to Raphael that launched his career; his copy of the *Galatea* so impressed the Roman patrician Marcello Sacchetti that he took the young artist into his household in 1623. In the service of the Sacchetti family Pietro gave the first proofs of his genius in painting and architecture.

In the Palazzo Sacchetti Pietro also met Cardinal Francesco Barberini, Pope Urban VIII's nephew, who became his lifelong patron. Through Barberini he obtained his early important commission as fresco painter in S. Bibiana. Simultaneously he received the patronage of Cassiano del Pozzo, Cardinal Francesco Barberini's connoisseur secretary, who employed a coterie of young and promising artists to produce for his collection copies of all the remains of antiquity. Pietro was over 26 years old when his contact with the "right" circle swept him to success and fame. From then on his career can easily be followed. While more can probably be added regarding his early development, "it will remain a fact of some significance that, whereas we can follow the unfolding of Bernini's talent year by year from his precocious beginnings, in Cortona we are almost suddenly faced with a distinctly individual manner in painting, and even more astonishingly, in architecture, though his training in this field can have been only rather superficial" (Wittkower, 152).

From the mid-1620's until his death Pietro had major architectural and pictorial commissions in production simultaneously, and he was "the only 17th century artist capable of such a tour-de-force" (Wittkower, 153). He reached the zenith of his artistic power and fame within ten years of obtaining his first major commissions. Acknowledging his distinction, his colleagues elected him *Principe* of the Accademia di San Luca for four straight years (1634–38). All of his major achievements involved religious themes. Among his greatest were the reconstruction of the Church of SS. Luca e Martina (1635–50) and the decoration of the Gran Salone of the Palazzo Barberini (1633–39). In addition to the many buildings he designed and decorated, he left plans for others, including the Louvre and Palazzo Pitti in Florence. The art historian Giuliano Briganti describes no less than 152 frescoes and easel paintings by Pietro da Cortona.

"There is no doubt that among Italian painters he must be considered the most influential personality of his generation, and this pre-eminence was recognized by his own contemporaries. His attitudes as well as his forms of expression were in harmony both with the new sense of grandeur and richness of the contemporary Catholic world, and with the spirit of absolutism then establishing itself among the monarchs of Europe. . . . Behind his formal eloquence there lies a sense of universal participation, a new vision of nature, that was one of the positive achievements of the Seicento. Pietro da Cortona changed the course of Italian painting markedly" (Briganti in the *Encyclopedia of World Art*, XI, 355–56).

How do the *Tabulae anatomicae* fit into this illustrious career in painting and architecture? Why were they published 72 years after the artist's death and perhaps over 100 years after their execution? For whom did Pietro make the studies? These questions have not been completely answered. It has been thought that the anatomical studies traditionally attributed to Pietro da Cortona were a project of his early years, before his sweep to fame in the 1620's. The date of 1618 has been assigned, partially based on the notion that 1618 can be read in an erased state on plates 1 and 4; however, in the copies of the first edition (1741) that we have examined, while it is clear that a date has been erased, it has been far too faint to be legible. The 1788 second editiion, the last until now, gives the 1618 date in its introduction; if the date had been erased from the plates in the eighteenth century for publication at that time, there is a good chance that the year given in the introduction represents the actual date of composition. This date also tallies well with the career of the presumed engraver, Luca Ciamberlano (b. 1580), whose monogram is found on plates 1 and 4, the plates from which the date has been erased (the monogram does not show up clearly on plate 1 in the copy reproduced here).

As to the identity of Pietro's anatomical collaborator, several propositions have been made, from the well-known anatomist, lecturer and textbook writer Johann Vesling (1598–1649) to the surgeon Nicolas Larchée (Lache, Larche), at whose dissections in Rome Poussin reputedly studied around 1625. Nothing appears to be recorded about Larchée in any of the standard reference sources in the history of medicine. His possible collaboration with Pietro da Cortona will be further discussed below.

No account has been given in the standard art-historical studies on Pietro da Cortona regarding the circumstances surrounding the publication of the *Tabulae anatomicae*. Their appearance in the eighteenth century was most certainly due in part to Pietro's reputation, which was very high at the time. The publication was undertaken by Gaetano Petrioli, surgeon to Victor Amadeus II of Sardinia, who had also come into possession and editorship of the celebrated anatomical plates of Bartolommeo Eustachi (c. 1505–74) after the papal physician Giovanni Maria Lancisi (1654–1720) had discovered and published them in 1714. Petrioli prepared the first edition of Pietro's anatomical plates by adding a commentary, as well as the small accessory figures in the margins, derived from Andreas Vesalius, Giulio Casserio and others. Because plates 21–26 are stylistically different from the rest, they are considered to have also been added. Petrioli's edition, which came out in 1741, is very rare today; it is the plates from a copy of this edition that are here reproduced.

These plates deal chiefly with muscles, nerves and blood vessels, with the nerves everywhere emphasized, leading to the conclusion that the book that they were originally intended to illustrate was to be a neurology text, and not an anatomy for artists or other general anatomy. The highly dramatic engravings and their landscape backgrounds are, nevertheless, consistent with Pietro da Cortona's artistic style. It must have been an interesting challenge for the young artist to synthesize the requirements of anatomical representation with his personal vision.

How Pietro met this challenge can fortunately now be studied not only from the plates but also from what are considered to be his original drawings, recently rediscovered by Dr. Helen Brock and Martin Kemp at the University of Glasgow. Up until very recently, the whereabouts of this vital link between Pietro da Cortona and the posthumously published *Tabulae anatomicae* attributed to him was quite forgotten. In fact, its very existence was obscured in the standard literature, where the suite of *drawings* was misrepresented as a suite of *plates* (see Haller, II, 752, and Choulant, 235). These drawings were given to the celebrated obstetrician, anatomist, art patron, connoisseur and collector/bibliophile William Hunter (1718–1783), who first brought the attention of the world to the anatomical drawings of Leonardo da Vinci at Windsor Castle. In fact, an unpublished letter written by Hunter in 1773, which appears to be the first written notice of the Leonardos, also contains a reference to the Pietro da Cortona drawings, which Hunter had obtained in 1772 from Sir William Hamilton, the famous archaeologist and diplomat then serving as British ambassador to the Kingdom of Naples.

The drawings that Hunter possessed, and that were left as his legacy in the Hunterian Library in Glasgow, represent twenty of the plates published in the *Tabulae anatomicae*, numbers 1–19 and 27, leaving out 21–26, which have traditionally been seen as additions. Of these twenty, all but the drawing for plate 11 have the appearance of drawings being progressively worked on with a view toward engraving, and not copies made after the fact. Number 11, the exception, may have been added on loss of the original; Hunter speculated that the drawing for number 20 should also have been part of the group, but must have been lost. The drawings were executed in black chalk, pen and ink, sepia wash and white heightening on buff paper tinted with gray wash. The outlines of the figures have been incised, sometimes cut sharply, in a manner consistent with transfer to a metal plate for engraving. In addition, the volume of drawings still bears, in the front, an Italian-language note that Hunter considered to be in an "old" (i.e., seventeenth-century) hand. Translated, this reads: "Twenty anatomical studies done by Pietro da Cortona at the S. Spirito Hospital in Rome, with the aid of the famous surgeon Nicolo Lache [see Larchée, above]. And they are originals from the pen of Cortona." This relatively contemporary ascription of the *Tabulae anatomicae* provides the most solid piece of evidence to date on the lineage of these extraordinary anatomical illustrations. Of the fate of the original plates, no mention is made either in Choulant or Kemp or in the more recent illustrated monograph by Duhme, which reproduces Pietro da Cortona's series of anatomical drawings for the first time. Figures 1–4 in our edition reproduce the drawings that correspond to plates 4, 5, 12 and 13.

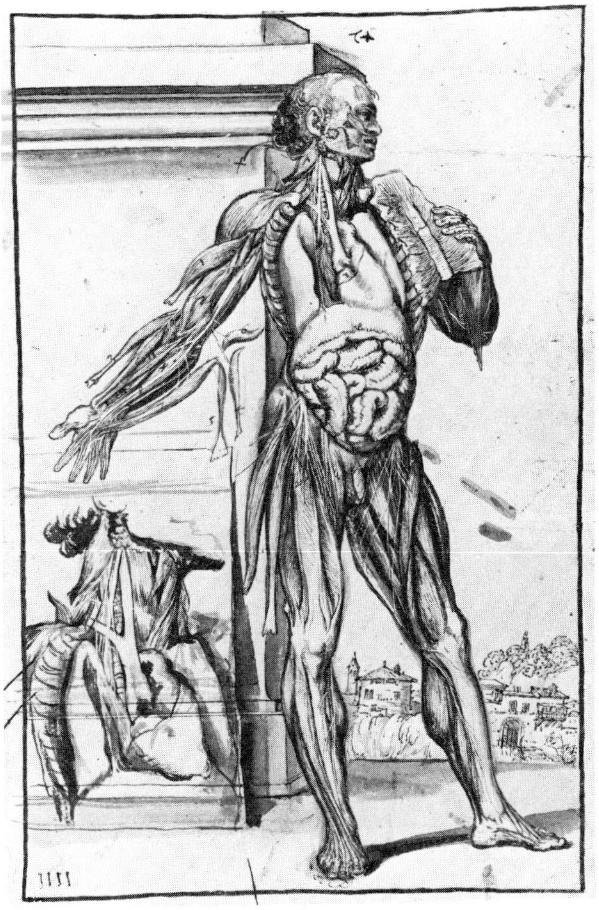

FIG. 1: Original drawing for plate 4.

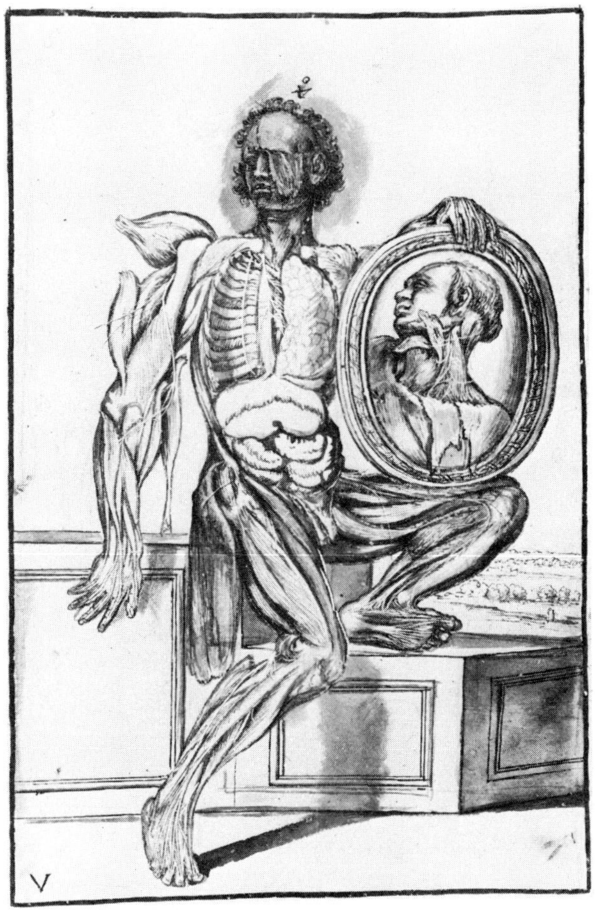

FIG. 2: Original drawing for plate 5.

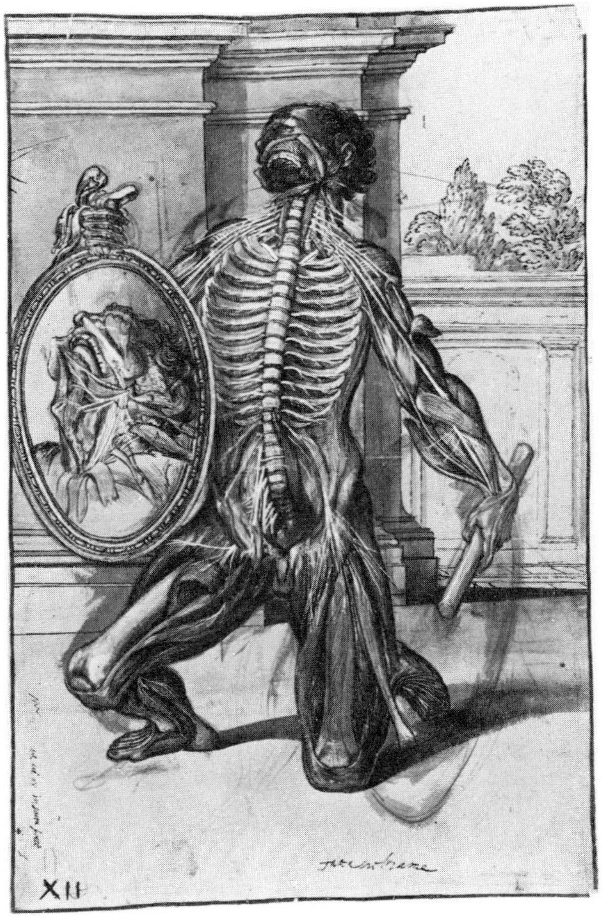

FIG. 3: Original drawing for plate 12.

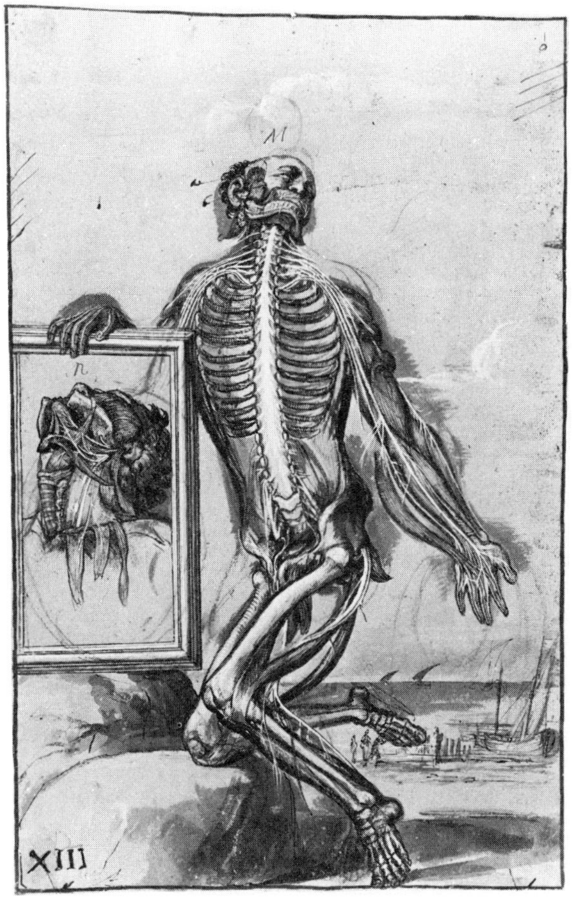

FIG. 4: Original drawing for plate 13.

Original drawing by Pietro da Cortona, all reproduced by courtesy of the University of Glasgow Library, Hunterian Collection, where the drawings are preserved.

Selected Bibliography

BRIGANTI, GIULIANO. *Pietro da Cortona o della pittura barocca.* Florence: Sansoni, 1962. Indispensable study of Pietro's work as a painter, including broad critical analysis and oeuvre catalogue.

CHOULANT, LUDWIG. *History and Bibliography of Anatomic Illustration.* Translated and annotated by Mortimer Frank. Further essays by Fielding H. Garrison *et al.* New York: Schuman's, 1945. Still the definitive work on this subject, originally published in German in 1852 at Leipzig.

DUHME, LÜDIKE. *Die Tabulae anatomicae des Pietro Berrettini da Cortona.* Cologne: Institut für Geschichte der Medizin, 1980.

FABBRINI, NARCISCO. *Vita del Cav. Pietro Berrettini da Cortona. Pittore ed architetto.* Cortona: Bimbi, 1896. Still useful though flawed, and not superseded.

HALLER, ALBRECHT. *Bibliotheca anatomica.* 2 vols. Zurich: Orell, 1774–77. Especially I, 340, 579; II, 752.

KEMP, MARTIN. "Dr William Hunter on the Windsor Leonardos and his Volume of Drawings attributed to Pietro da Cortona." *Burlington Magazine* **118** (1976), 144–48.

PIETRO DA CORTONA. *Tabulae anatomicae a celeberrimo pictore Petro Berrettini Cortonensi Delineatae . . . nunc primum prodeunt, et a Cajetano Petrioli . . . Notis illustratae.* Folio. [4], 84pp. 27 copperplates. Rome: Impensis Fausti Amidei . . . Ex Typographia Antonii de Rubeis. 1741. The first edition, with figures and text added by Petrioli.

. *Tabulae anatomicae ex archetypis egregii pictoris Petri Berrettini Cortonensis expressae . . . Alteram hanc editionem recensuit, nothas iconas expunxit, perpetuas explicationes adjecit Franciscus Petraglia.* . . . Folio. [16], 104pp. 27 copperplates. Rome: Impensis Venantii Monaldini . . . excud. Johann. Zempel. 1788. The second edition, with the figures added to the margins by Petrioli removed and with new text supplied by Petraglia.

WITTKOWER, RUDOLF. *Art and Architecture in Italy. 1600 to 1750.* 2nd rev. ed. London: Penguin Books, 1965. Gives on pp. 152–68 the best modern summary of Pietro da Cortona's achievements, especially in architecture.

The Anatomical Plates of
Pietro da Cortona

PLATE 1

FIGURE 1: Blood vessels and nerves associated with the outermost muscle layer.
FIGURE 2: Blood vessels and nerves of the peritoneum.
FIGURE 3: Abdomen with muscles removed and peritoneum folded back.

TABVLA .I.

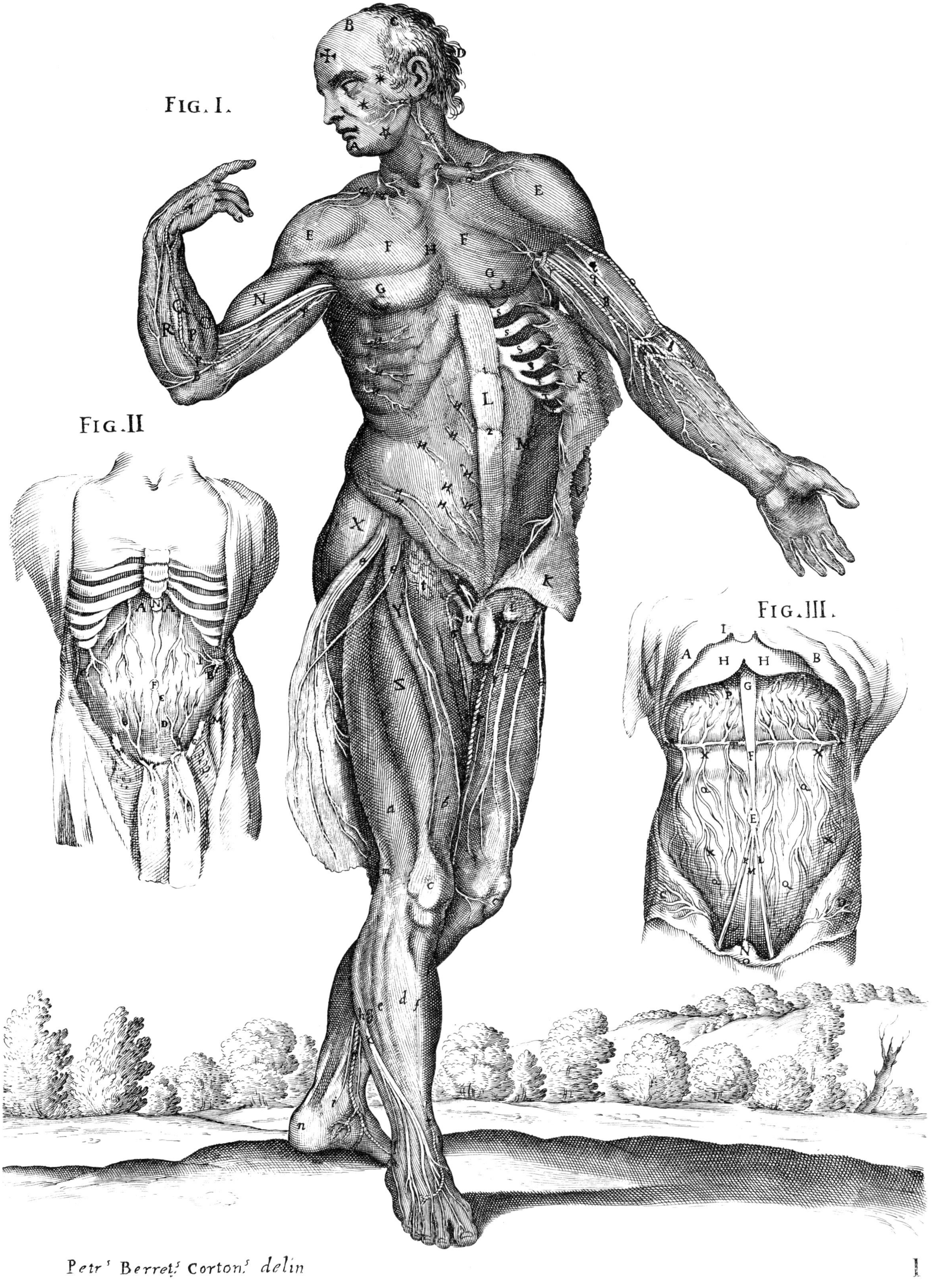

Petr' Berret. Corton. delin

PLATE 2

FIGURE 1: Outer muscles detached; blood vessels and nerves of the next layer.
FIGURE 2: Omentum folded upward, revealing the intestines.
FIGURE 3: Omentum and its blood vessels.
FIGURE 4: Abdominal viscera fully exposed.

TAB. II.

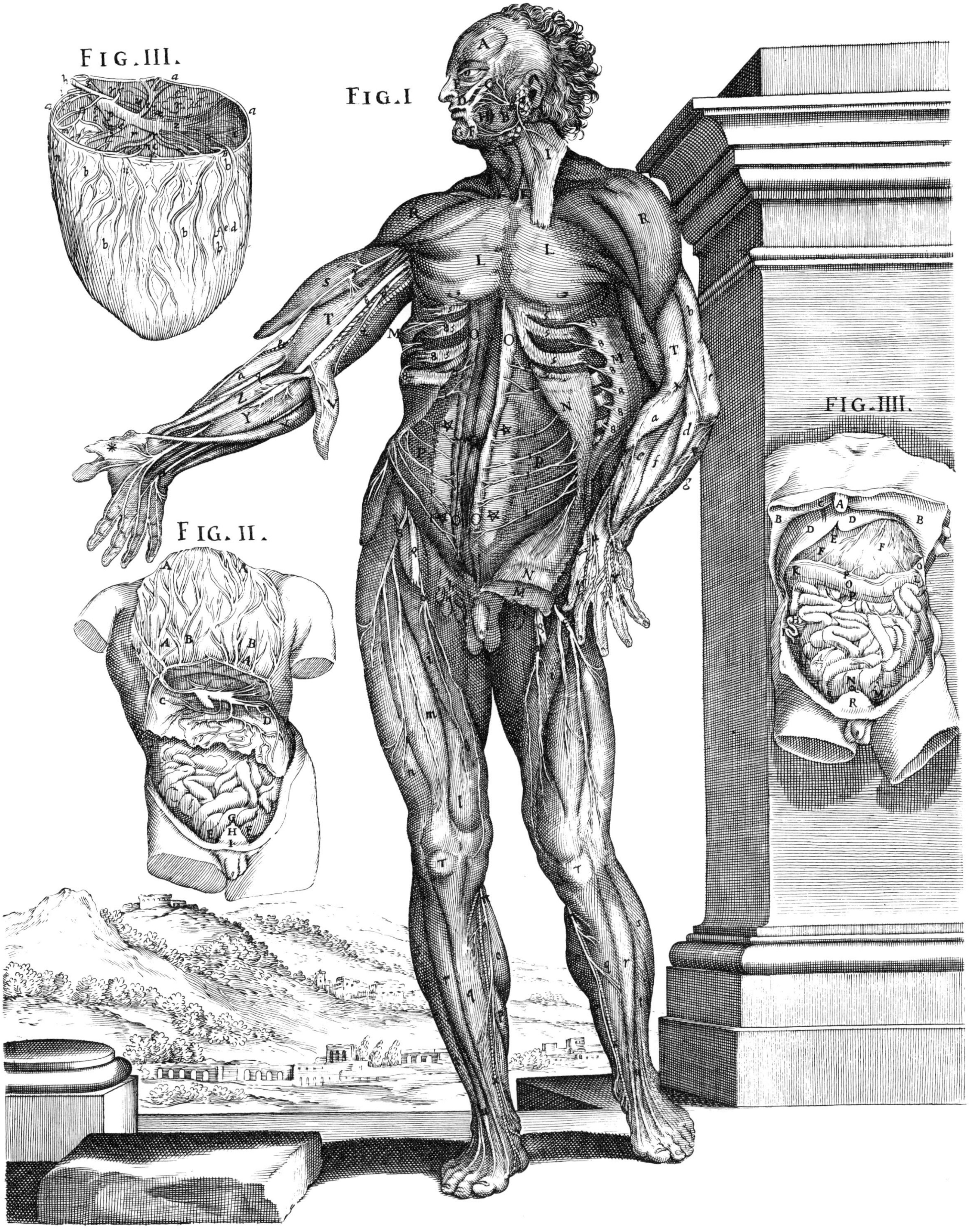

PLATE 3

FIGURE 1: Nerves seen after removal of some muscles and all abdominal viscera.
FIGURE 2: Nerves, veins and tendons of the back of the hand.
FIGURE 3: Nerves of the neck.
FIGURE 4: Omentum and colon.
FIGURE 5: Colon.

TAB. III.

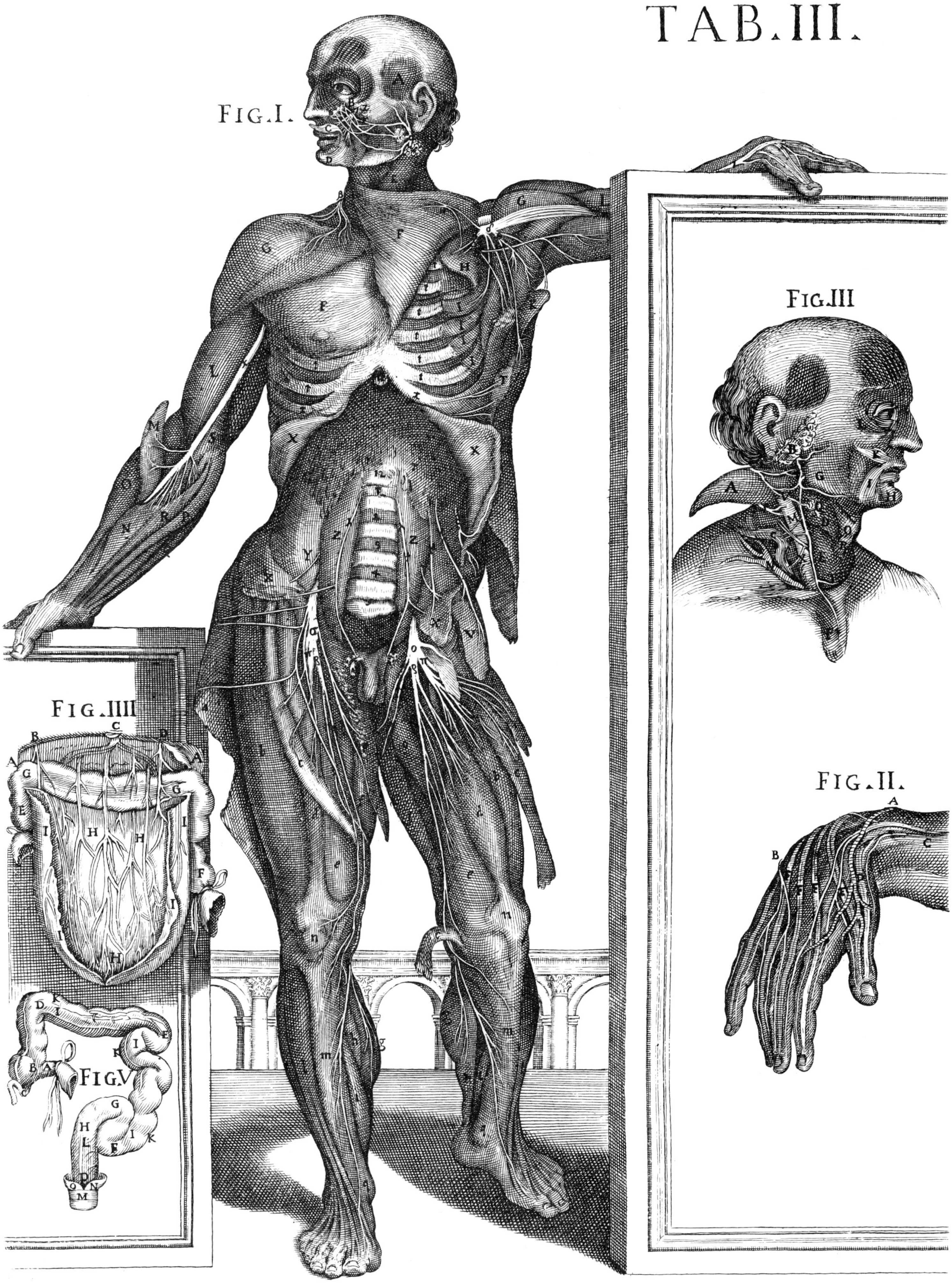

PLATE 4

FIGURE 1: Nerves of the thorax and abdomen.
FIGURE 2: Part of the intestines raised, displaying the mesentery.
FIGURE 3: Mesentery.

TAB. IIII.

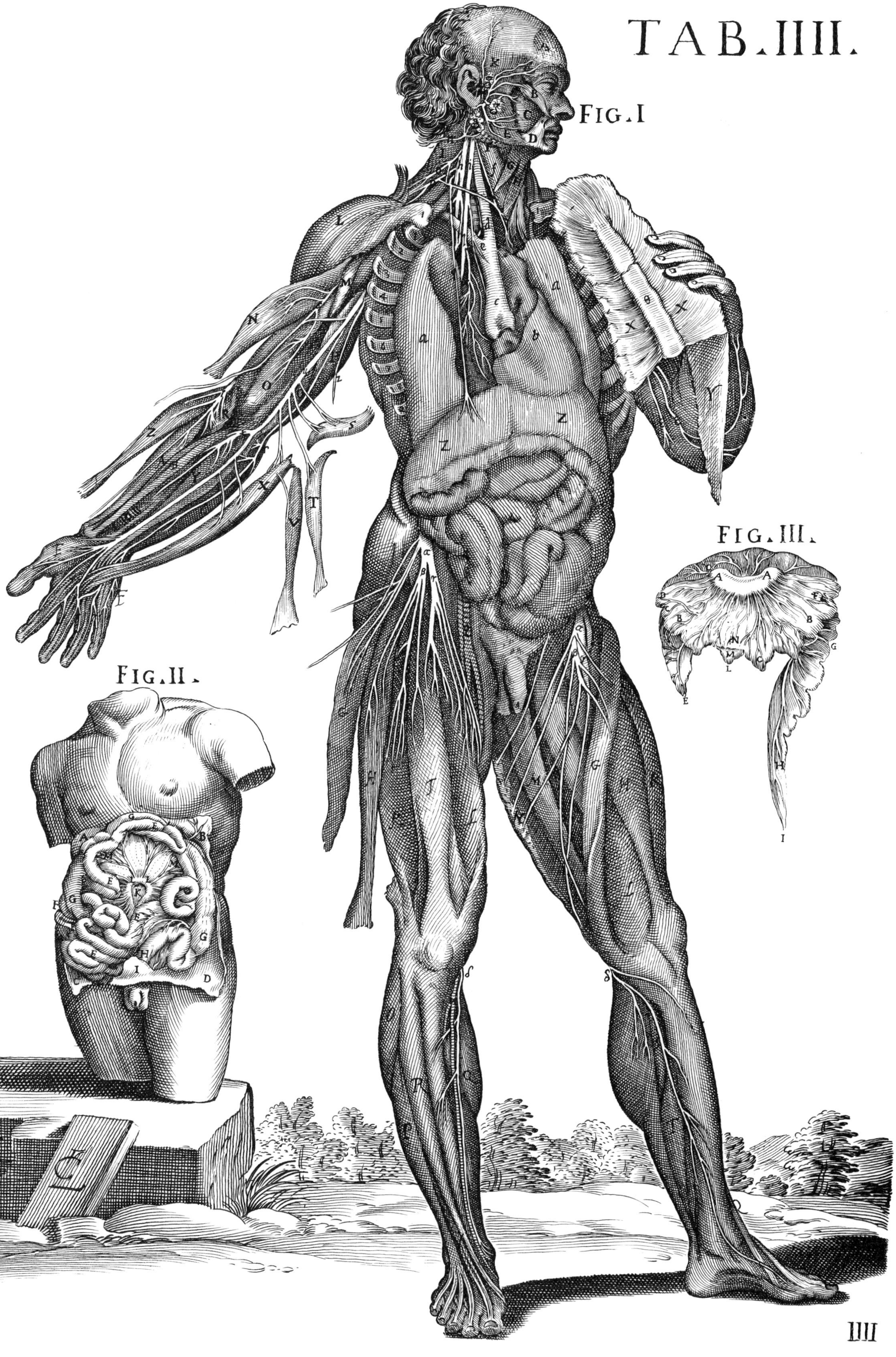

PLATE 5

FIGURE 1: Deep nerves of the limbs and thorax.
FIGURE 2: Nerves of the neck.
FIGURE 3: Abdominal viscera, showing their connection with the mesentery.
FIGURE 4: Stomach.

TAB. V.

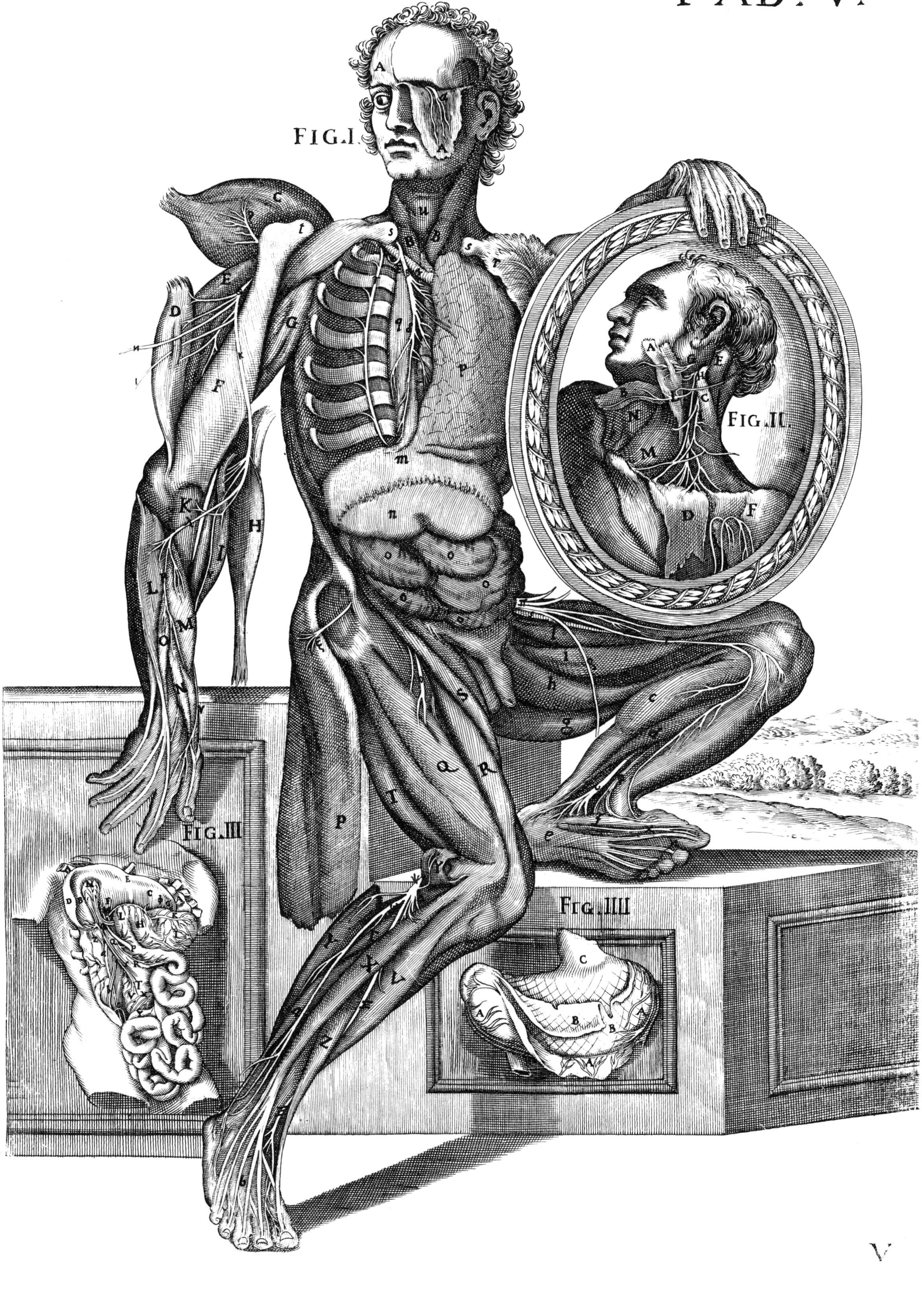

PLATE 6

FIGURE 1: Deep nerves of the limbs and thorax.
FIGURE 2: Rear view of the stomach with nerves and blood vessels.
FIGURE 3: Front view of the stomach with nerves and blood vessels.
FIGURE 4: Spleen with blood vessels.
FIGURE 5: Concave face of the spleen.
FIGURE 6: Convex face of the spleen.
FIGURE 7: Spleen incised to reveal its pulpy interior.
FIGURE 8: Convex face of the liver with a portion of the vena cava.

TAB. VI.

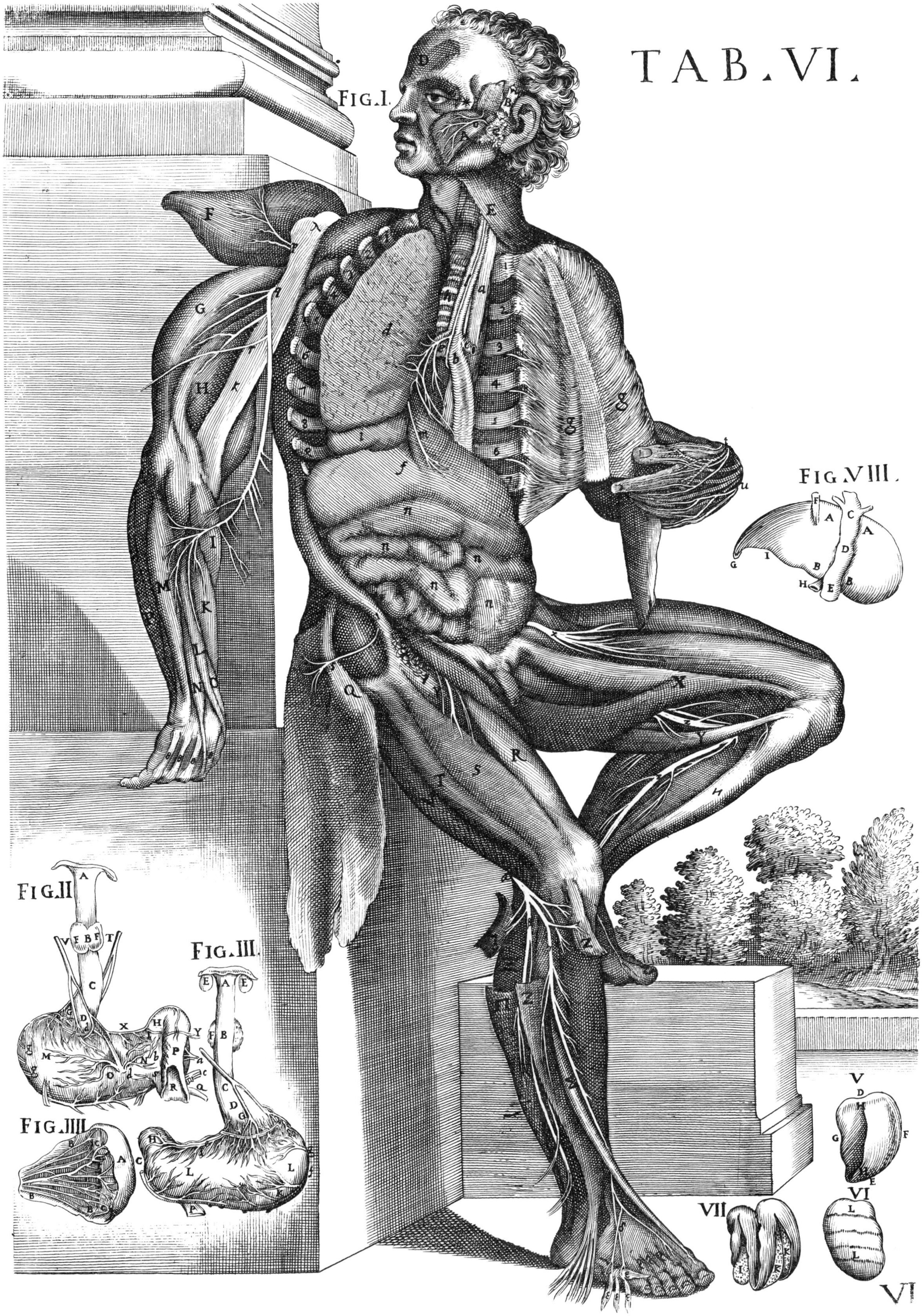

PLATE 7

FIGURE 1: Deep nerves of the limbs and thorax.
FIGURE 2: Abdomen after removal of the intestines.
FIGURE 3: Kidney.
FIGURE 4: Kidneys with blood vessels.
FIGURE 5: Section of a kidney.

TAB. VII.

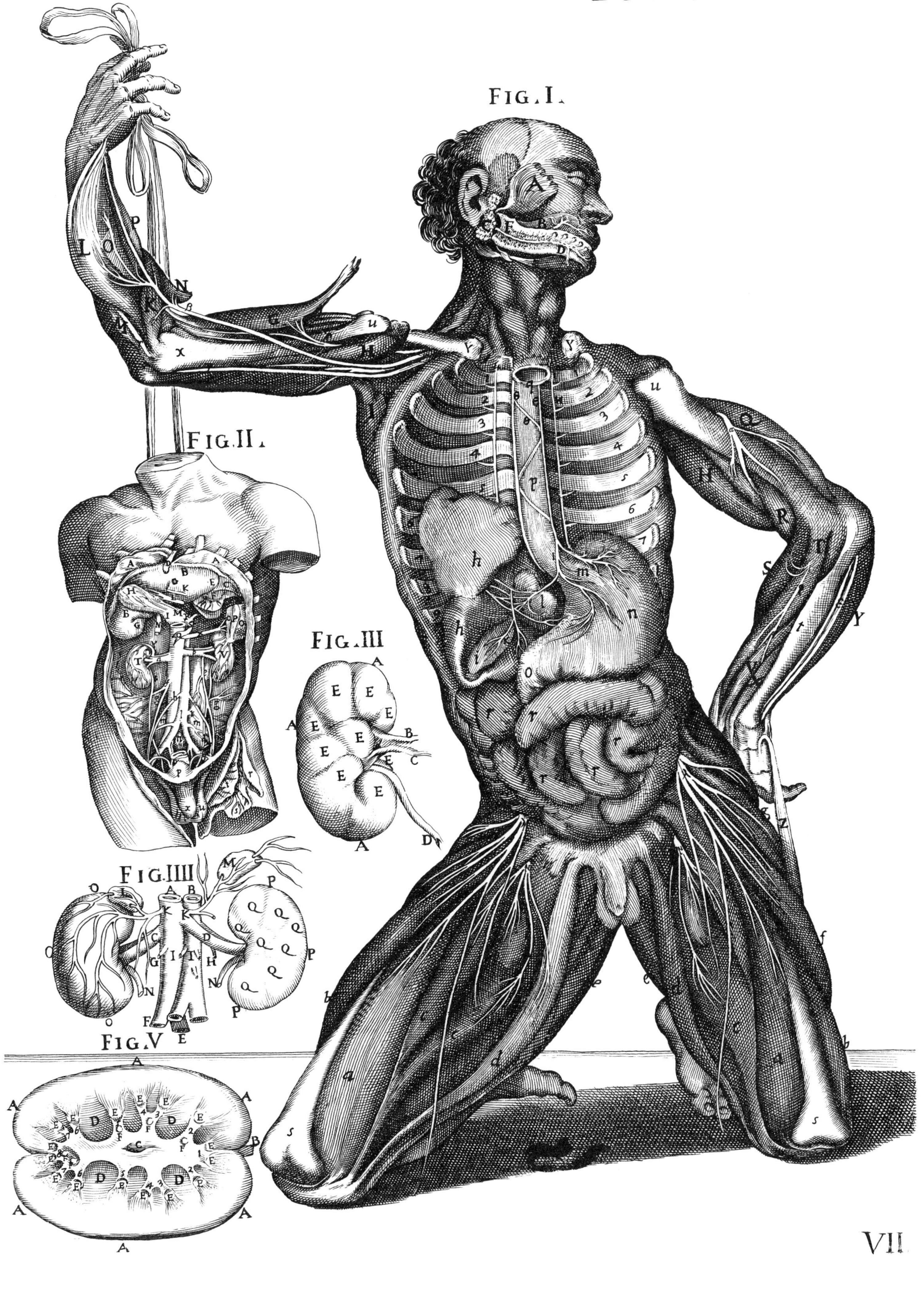

PLATE 8

FIGURE 1: Deep nerves of the limbs and thorax.
FIGURE 2: Male urogenital system in situ.
FIGURE 3: Male urogenital system, front view.
FIGURE 4: Male urogenital system, rear view.
FIGURE 5: Views of the testicle and epididymus.

TAB. VIII.

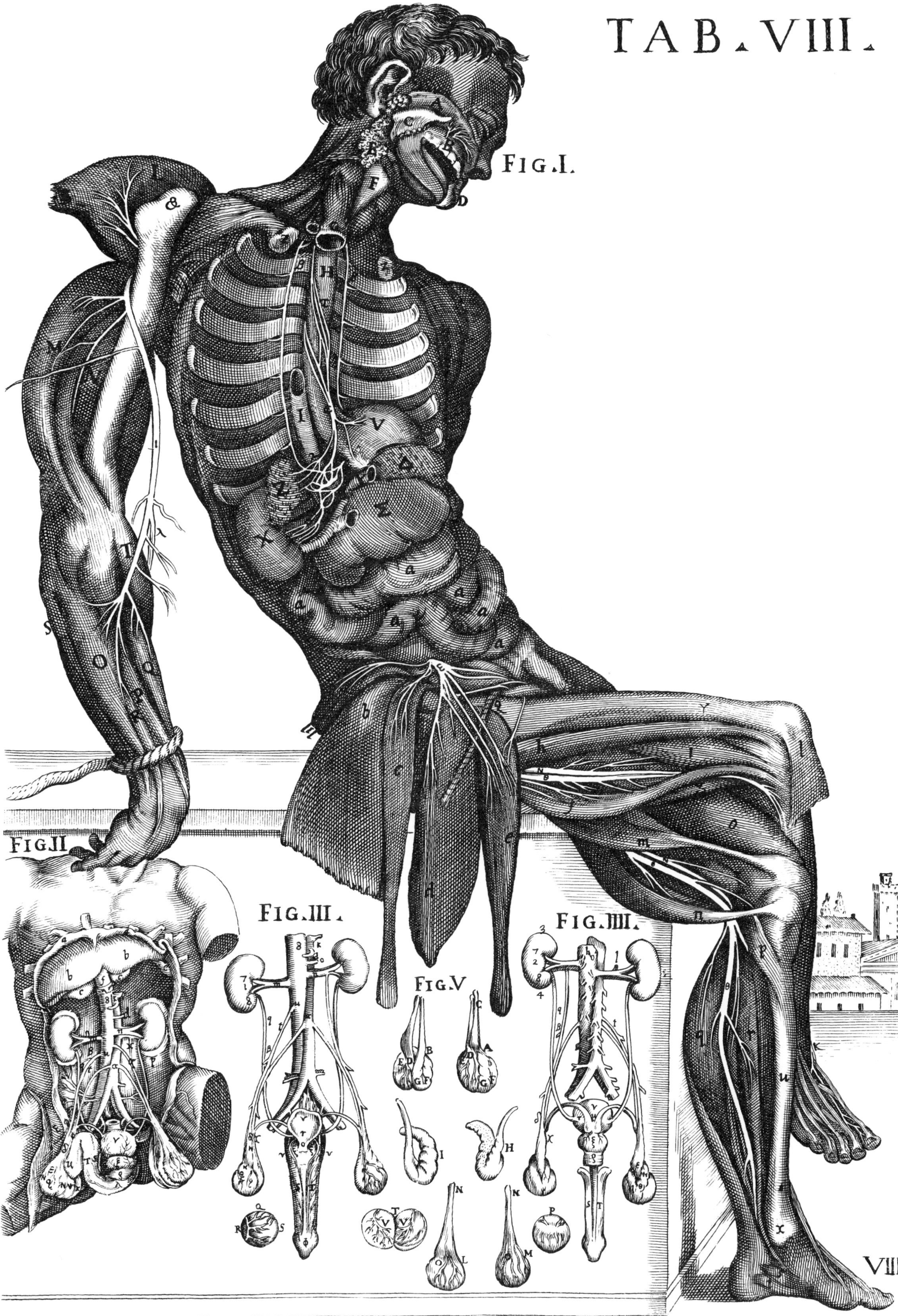

PLATE 9

FIGURE 1: Abdominal viscera pulled back to reveal deep blood vessels and nerves.
FIGURE 2: Thorax with the sternum and part of the ribs removed.
FIGURE 3: Heart flanked by the lungs.
FIGURE 4: Heart stripped of the pericardium.
FIGURE 5: Heart turned to the left side.
FIGURE 6: Heart turned to the right side.

TAB. IX.

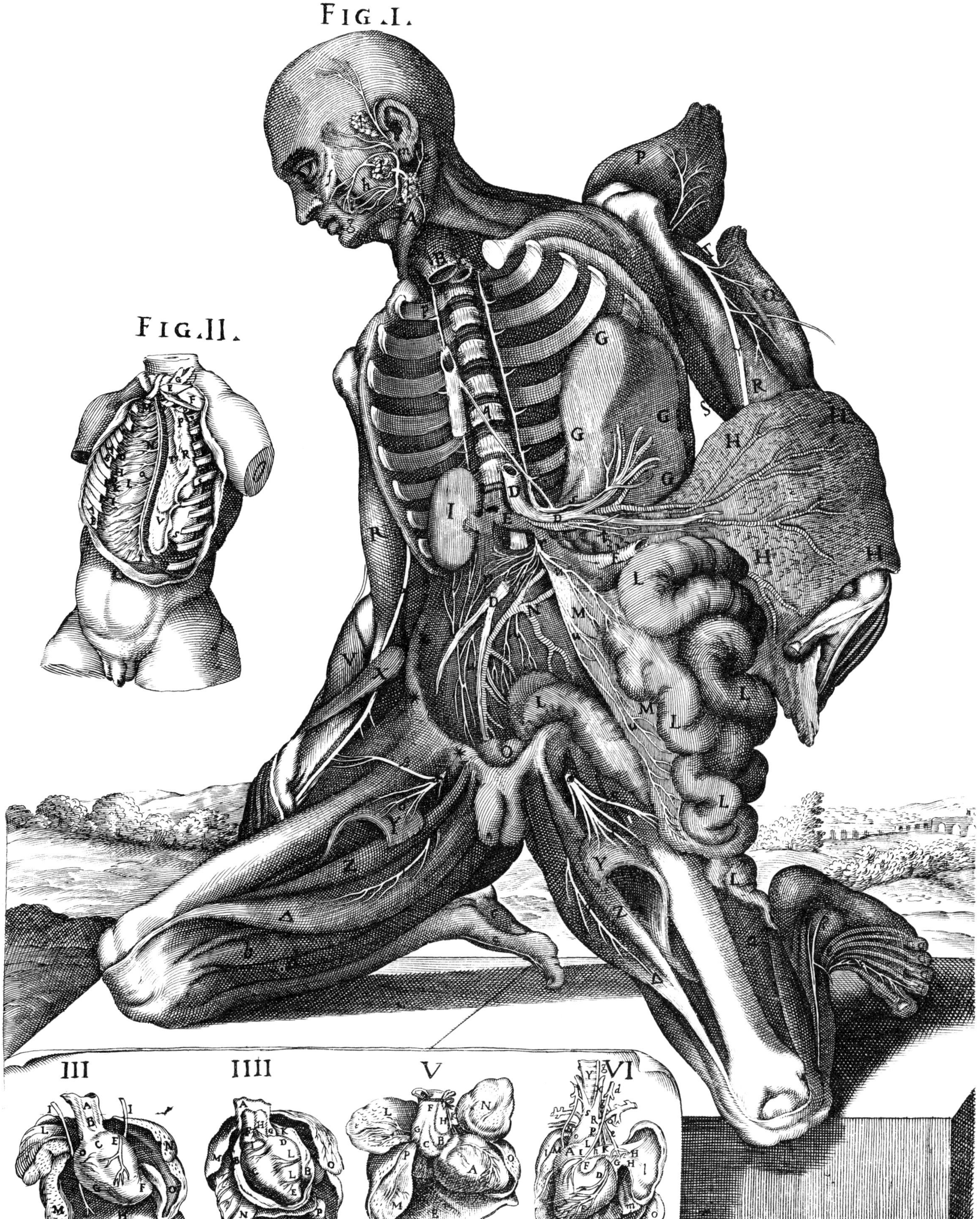

PLATE 10

FIGURE 1: Nerves seen after the removal of the abdominal and thoracic viscera.
FIGURE 2: Muscles of the neck.
FIGURE 3: Thorax opened, with the sternum lifted.
FIGURES 4–8: Several views and sections of the ventricles of the heart.
FIGURE 9: Front view of the lungs, with the heart removed.
FIGURE 10: Rear view of the lungs.

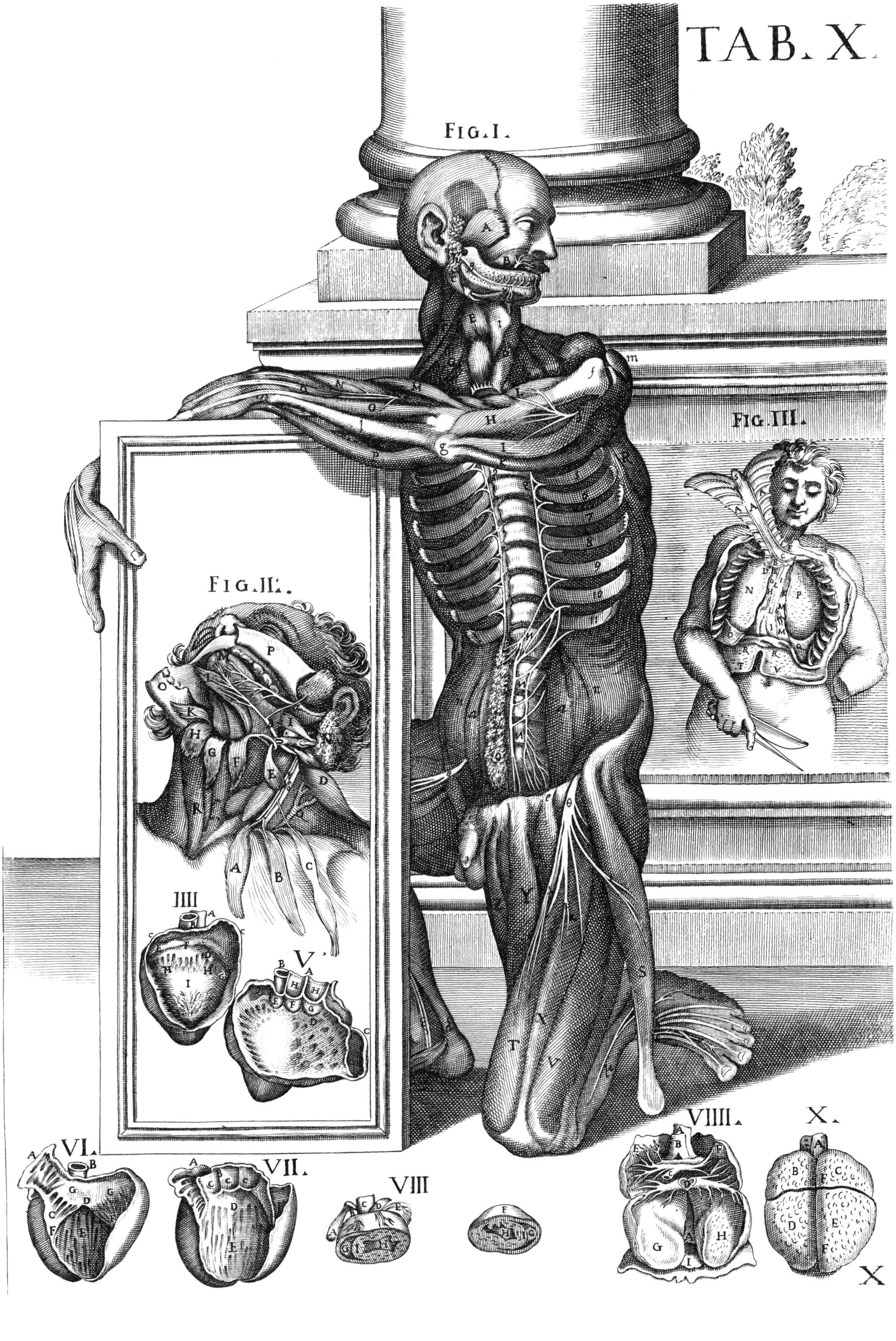
TAB. X.
FIG. I.
FIG. II.
FIG. III.
IIII
V
VI.
VII.
VIII
VIIII.
X.
X

PLATE 11

FIGURE 1: Nerves of the thorax, abdomen and limbs.
FIGURE 2: Muscles of the tongue and vicinity.
FIGURE 3: Cranium.
FIGURE 4: Larynx, lungs, heart and associated structures.

TAB. XI.

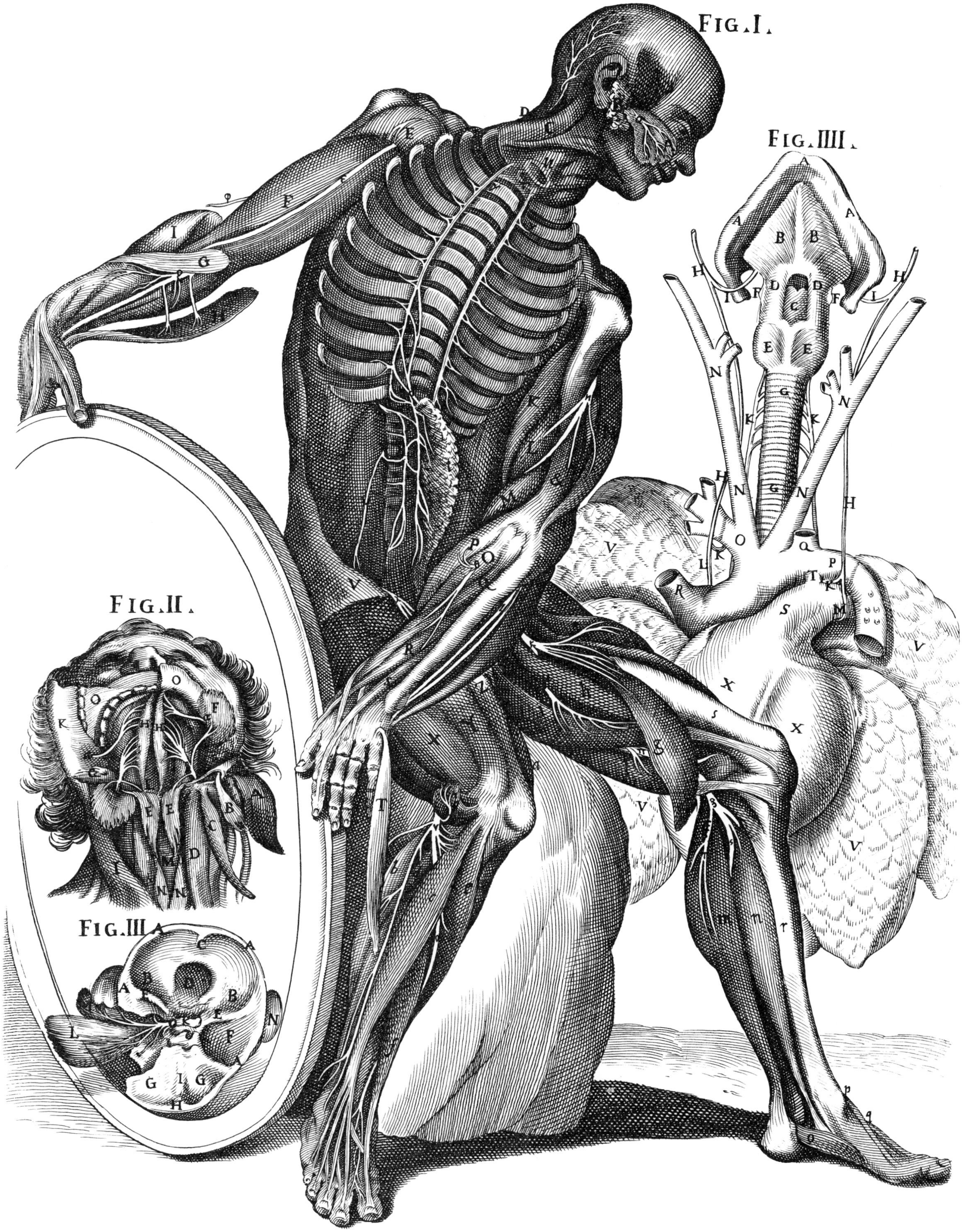

PLATE 12

FIGURE 1: Spinal nerves (the 31 pairs springing from the spinal cord).
FIGURE 2: Nerves of the tongue and vicinity.
FIGURE 3: Rear view of the larynx and trachea, with the esophagus.

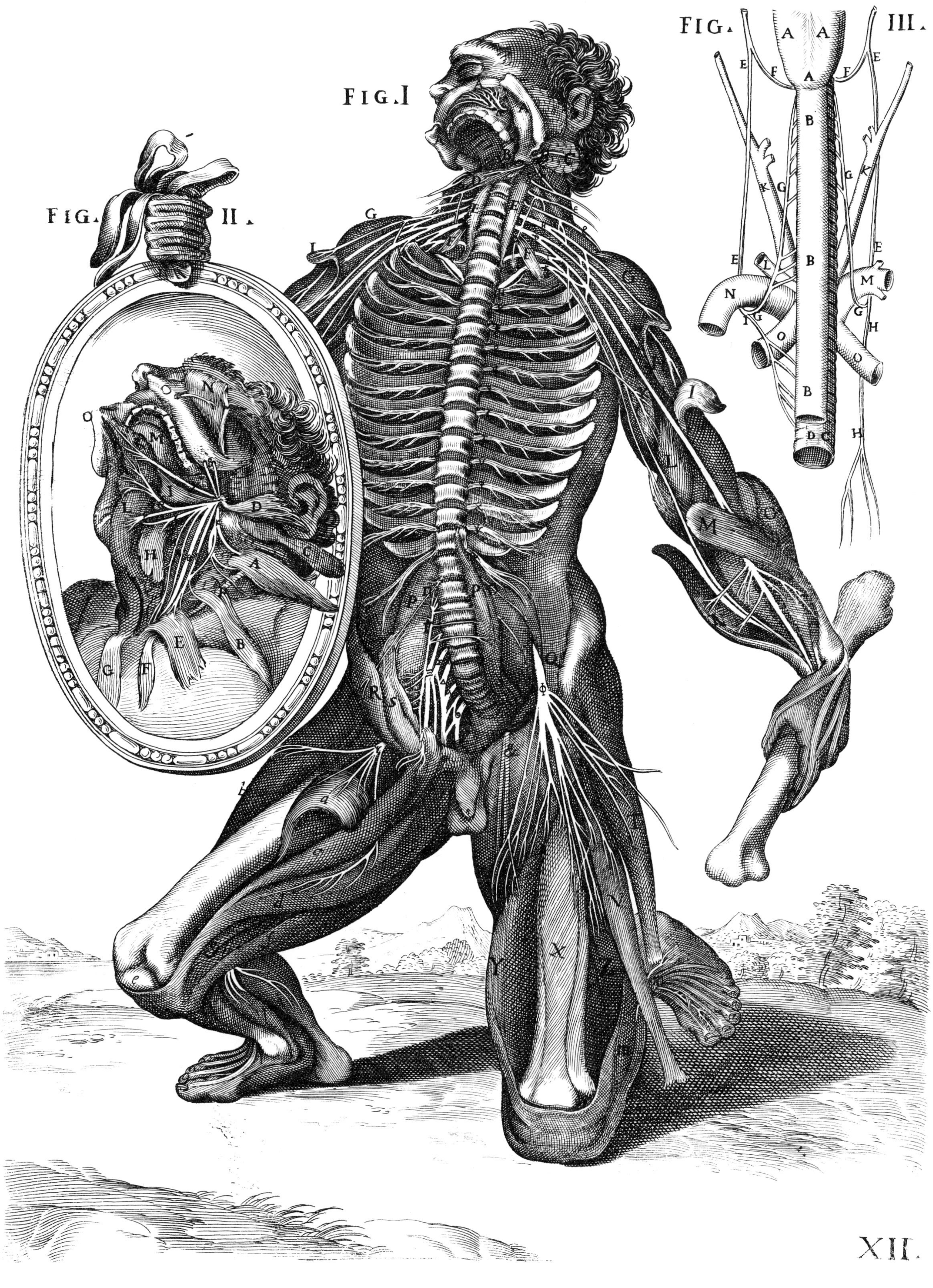
FIG. I
FIG. II.
FIG. III.

PLATE 13

FIGURE 1: Spinal cord as the source of the nerves of the neck, loins and limbs.
FIGURE 2: Nerves of the throat and tongue.
FIGURES: 3–5: Three views of the thyroid cartilage.
FIGURES: 6–11, 14 & 15: Various views of the cricoid cartilage.
FIGURES: 12 & 13: Epiglottis.
FIGURES 16 & 17: Arytenoid cartilage.

TAB. XIII.

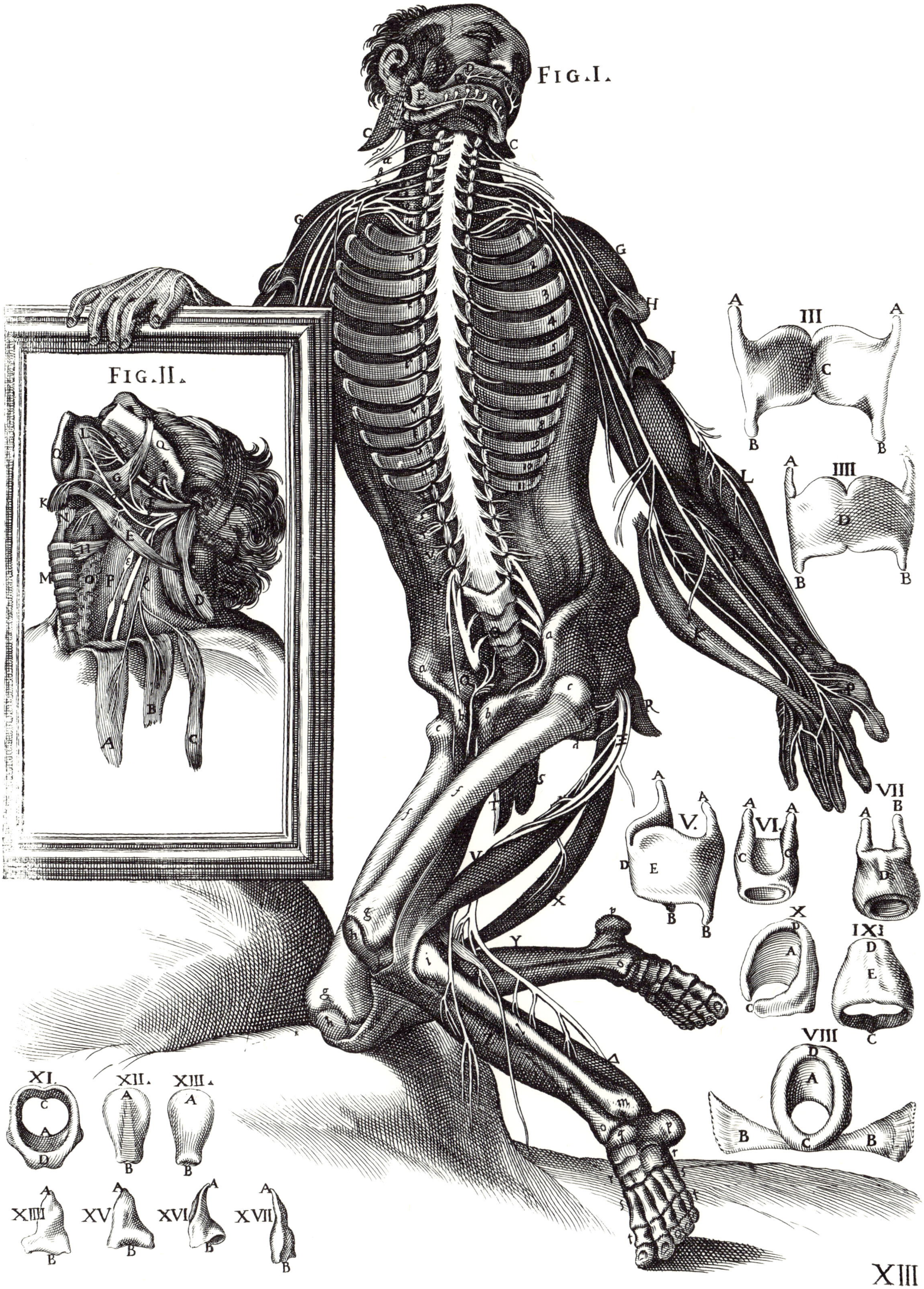
FIG. I.
FIG. II.
III
IIII
V.
VI
VII
VIII
IX
X
XI.
XII.
XIII.
XIIII
XV
XVI
XVII

PLATE 14

FIGURE 1: Sources of various nerves in the spinal cord.
FIGURE 2: Side view of the skull.
FIGURE 3: Bottom view of the skull.
FIGURE 4: Interior view of the lower part of the skull.
FIGURE 5: Interior view of the cranium.
FIGURE 6: Ethmoid bone.
FIGURES 7 & 8: Two views of the lower jaw.

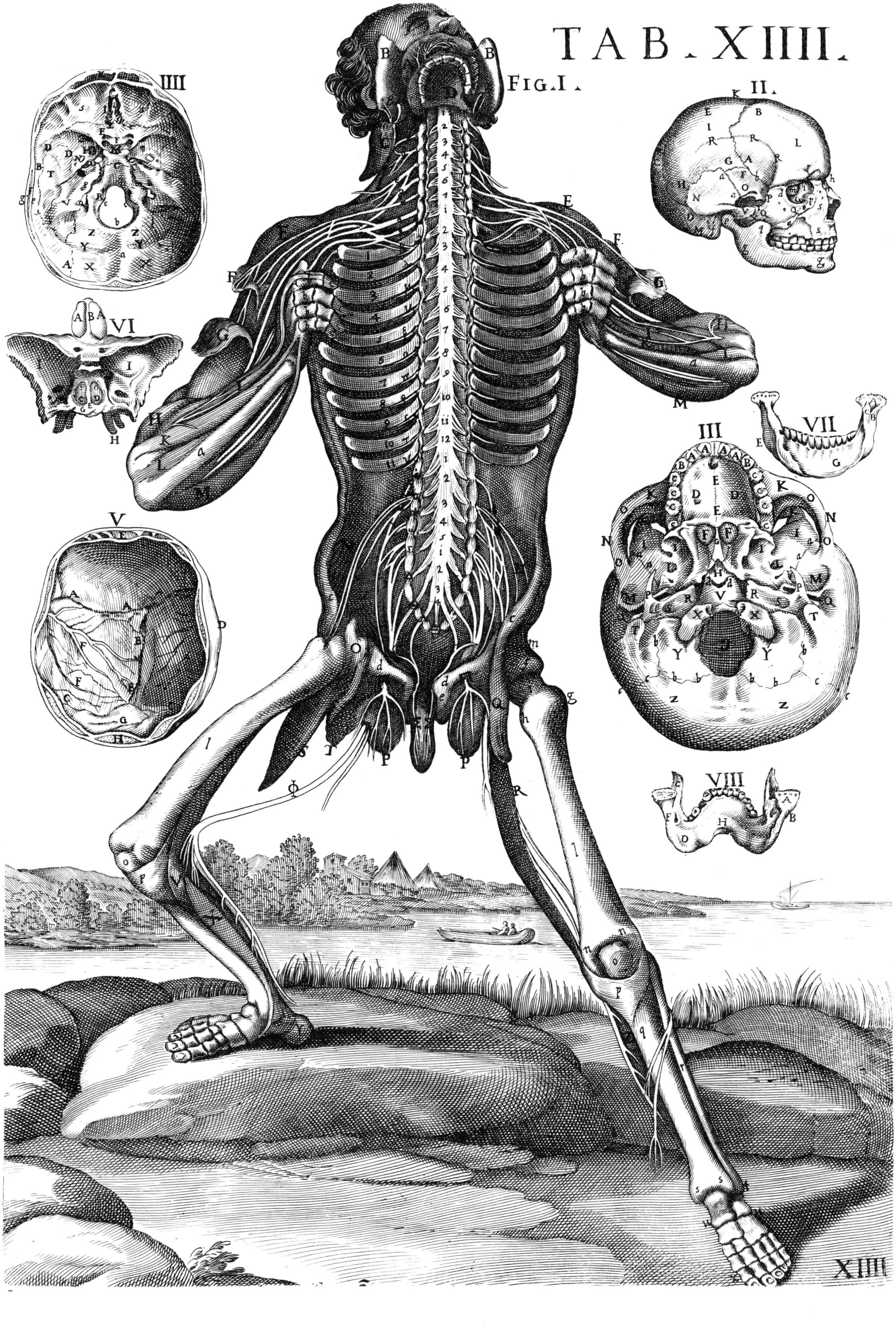
TAB. XIIII.
FIG. I.
II.
IIII
VI
VII
III
V
VIII
XIIII

PLATE 15

FIGURE 1: Superficial nerves seen from the rear.
FIGURE 2: Cerebrum covered by the dura mater.
FIGURE 3: Dura mater folded back to show the pia mater.
FIGURE 4: Pia mater folded back to show the cerebrum.

TAB. XV.

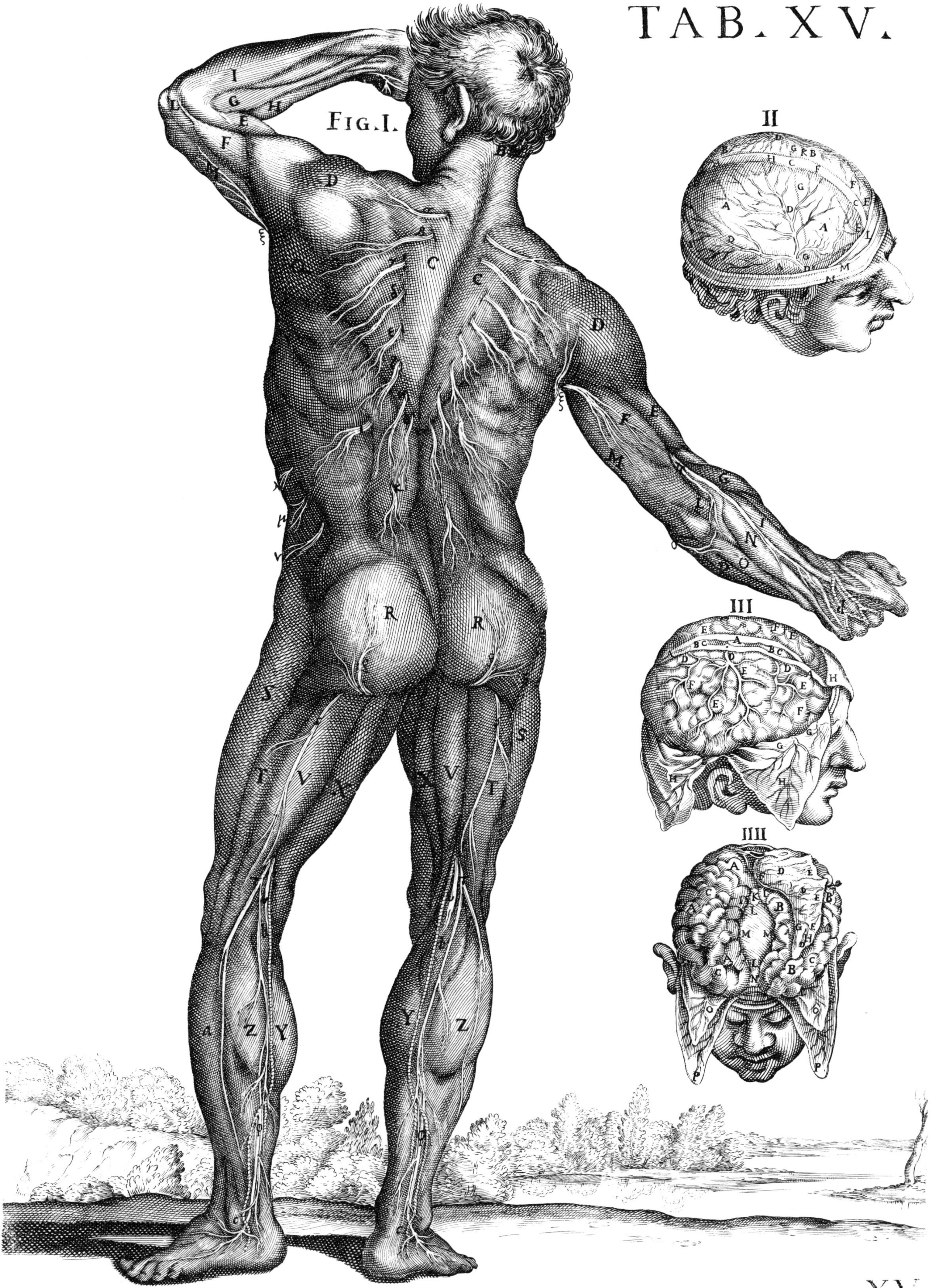

PLATE 16

FIGURE 1: Superficial nerves on the left side.
FIGURE 2: Dissection revealing the apophyses of the cervical and upper dorsal vertebrae.
FIGURES 3–6: Successive dissections of the cerebrum.

TAB. XVI.

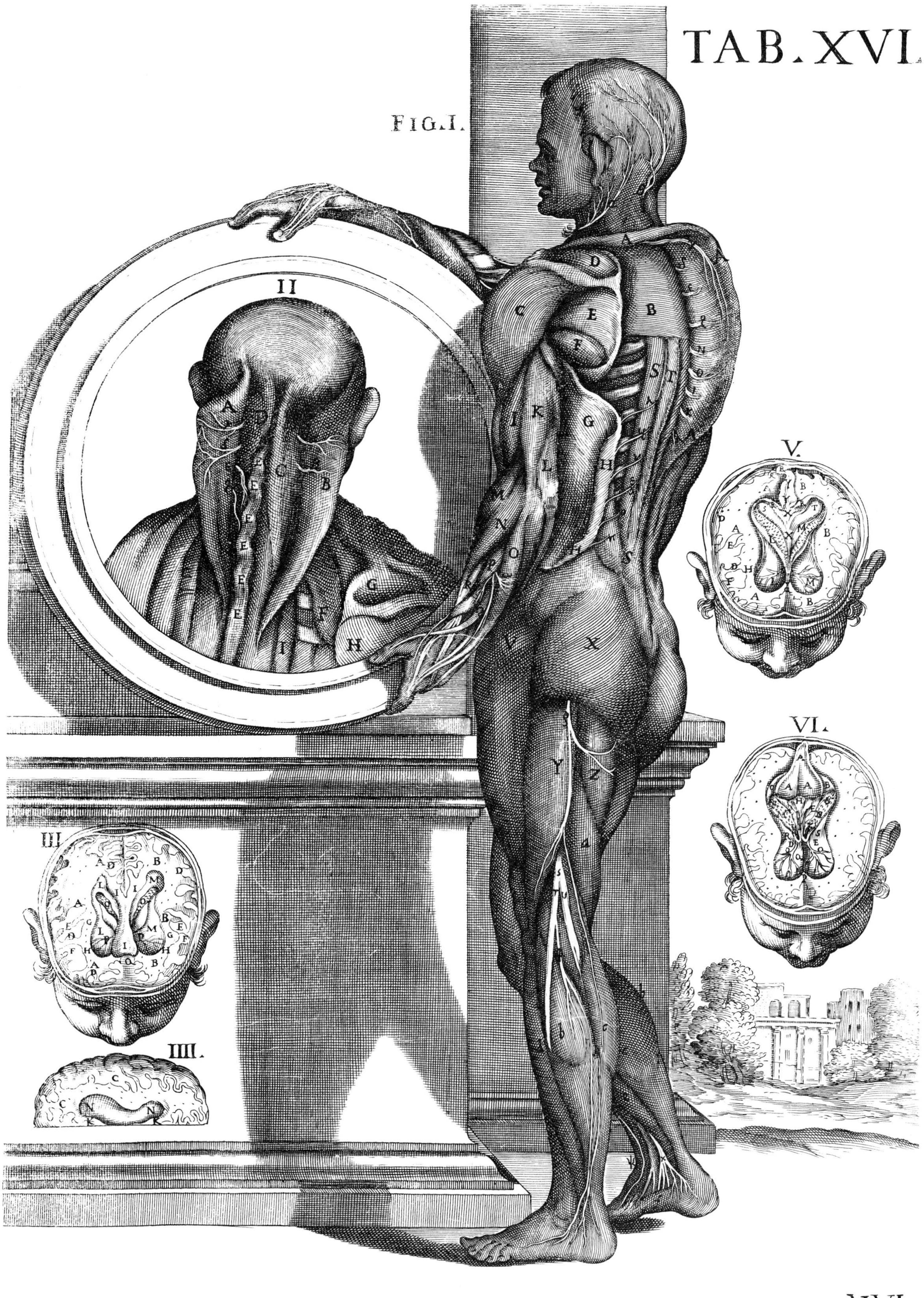

PLATE 17

FIGURE 1: Deep nerves seen from the rear.
FIGURE 2: Dissection of the brain revealing the cerebellum.
FIGURE 3: Cerebellum freed from the dura mater.
FIGURE 4: Cerebellum moved aside to reveal the medulla oblongata.
FIGURE 5: Medulla oblongata.
FIGURE 6: Bottom view of the cerebellum.

TAB.XVIII.

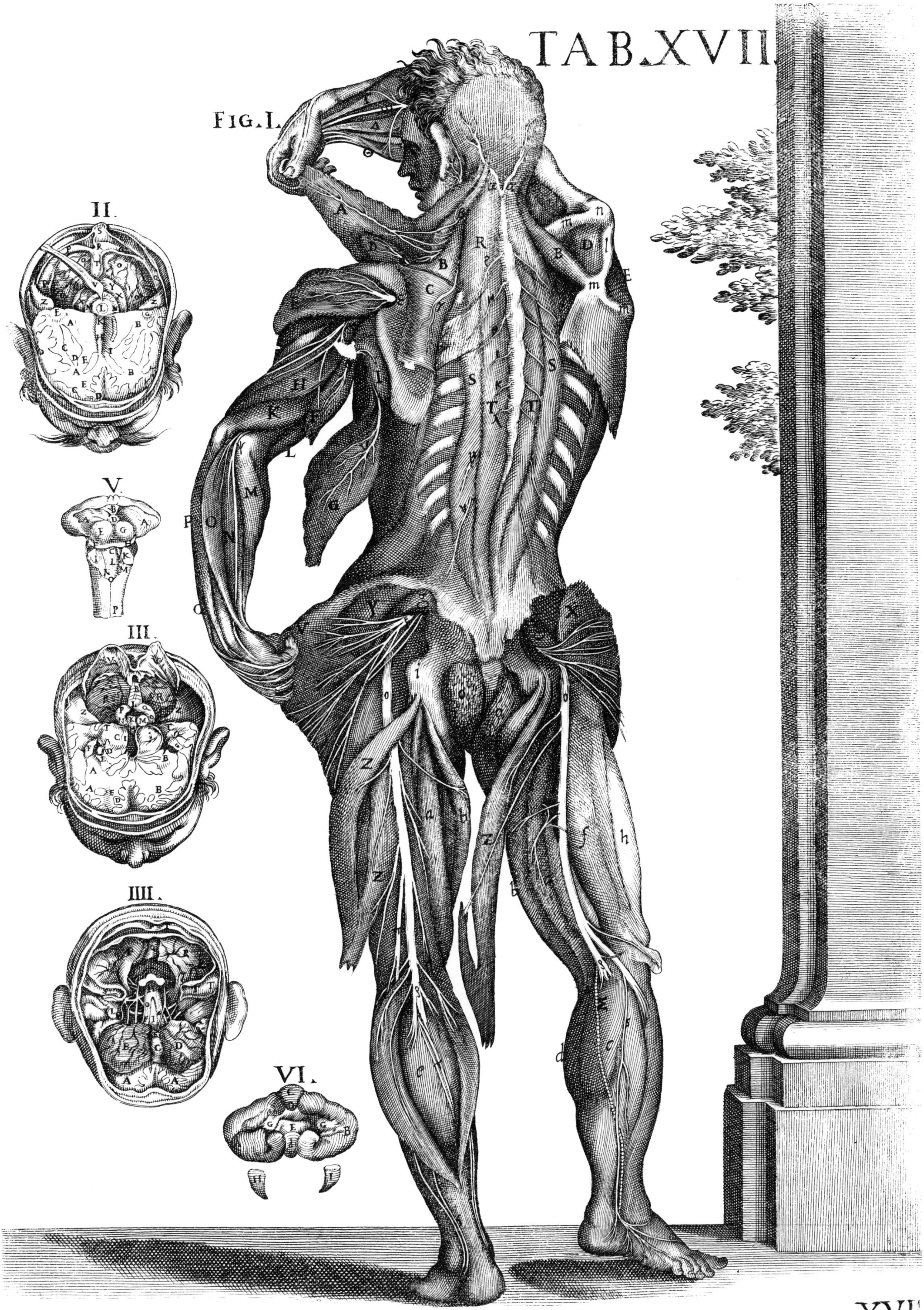

PLATE 18

FIGURE 1: Deep nerves seen from the rear.
FIGURE 2: Nerves of the left foot.
FIGURE 3: Cranial nerves.
FIGURE 4: Olfactory and optic nerves in situ.
FIGURE 5: Nerves springing from the medulla oblongata.

TAB. XVIII.

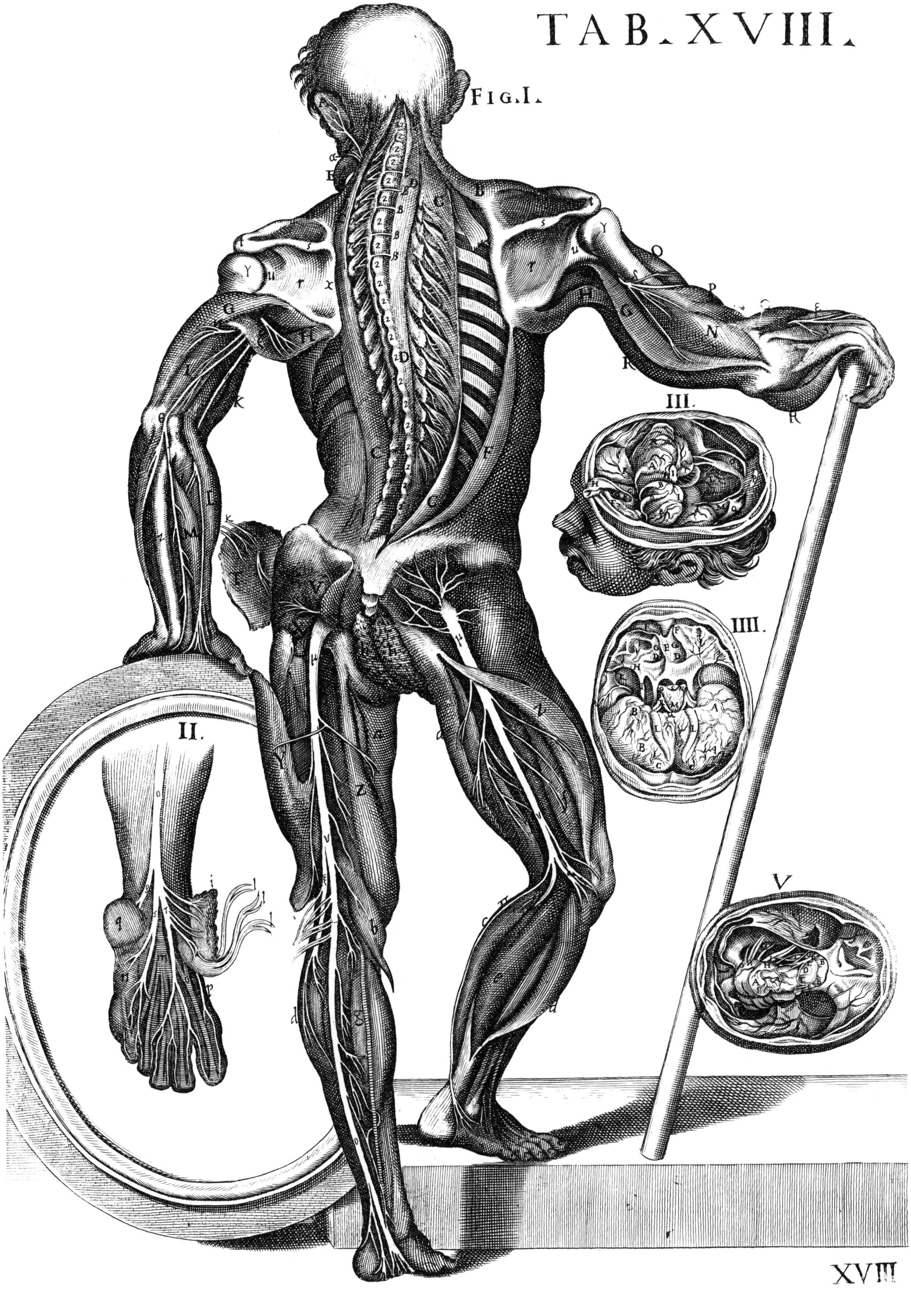

PLATE 19

FIGURE 1: Rear view of muscle/nerve connections.
FIGURE 2: Rear view of the nerves and muscles of the left leg.
FIGURE 3: Rear view of the cranium with supporting muscles.
FIGURE 4: Rear view of the cranium and upper vertebrae.
FIGURE 5: Three views of clavicles.
FIGURES 6 & 7: Three views of the scapula.
FIGURES 8 & 9: Hyoid bone.

TAB. XIX.

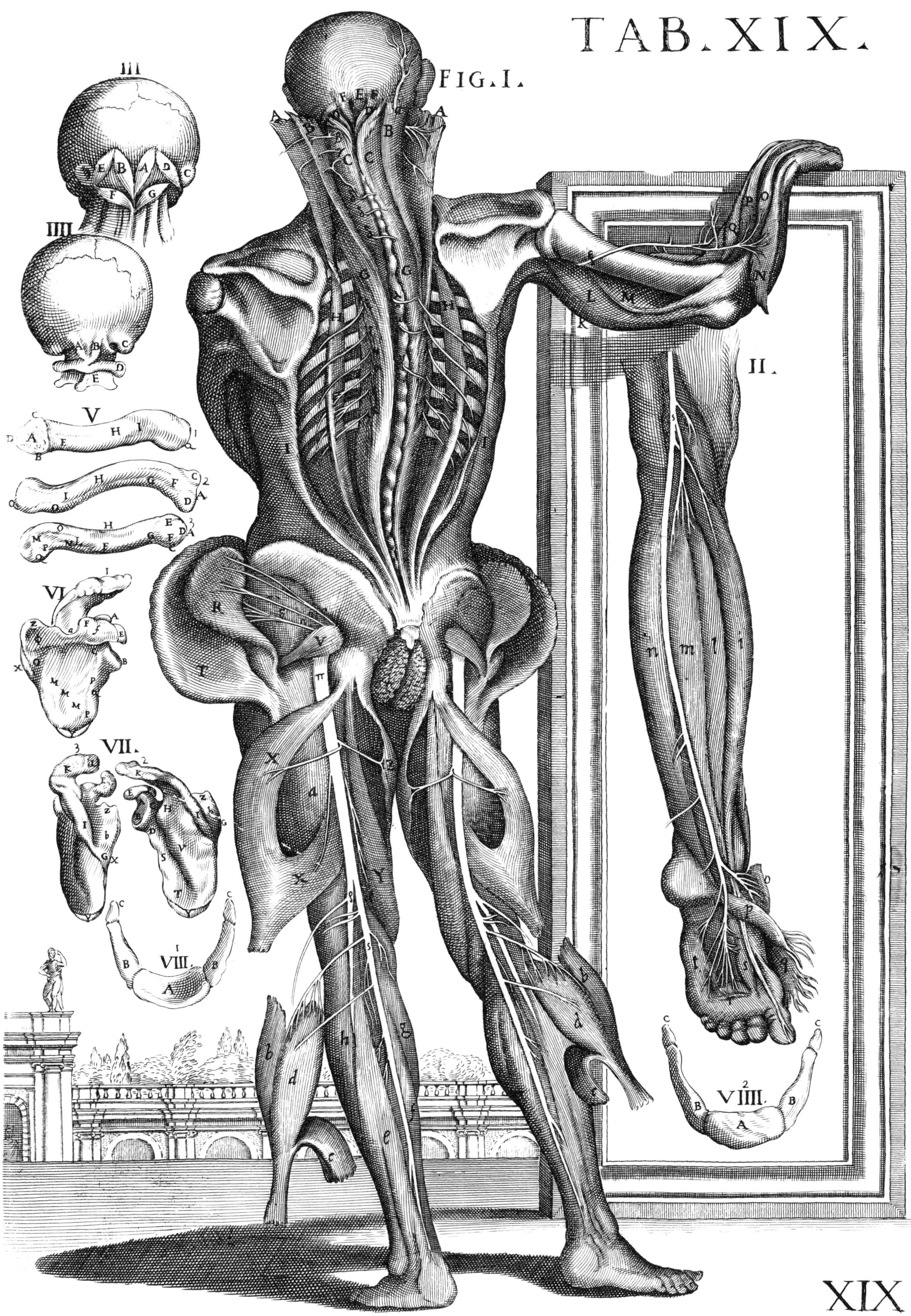

PLATE 20

FIGURE 1: Spinal column.
FIGURES 2 & 3: Humerus.
FIGURES 4 & 5: Ulna and radius.
FIGURES 6 & 7: Tibia and fibula.
FIGURES 8 & 9: Femur.
FIGURES 10–12: Ilium.
FIGURES 13 & 14: Bones of the hand.
FIGURES 15–18: Carpus.
FIGURES 17 *bis* & 19: Bones of the foot.
FIGURES 20–30: Various views of foot bones.

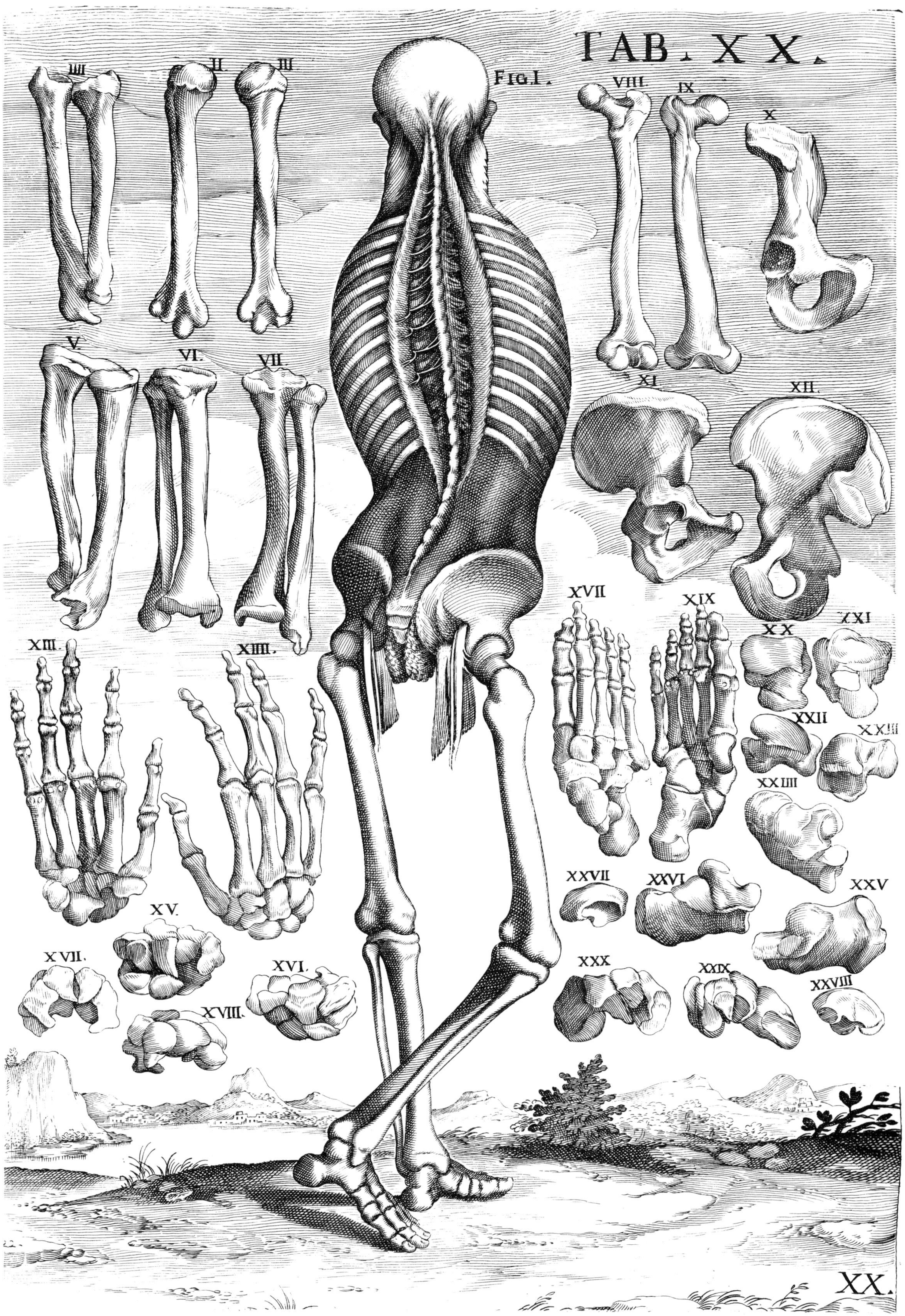
TAB. XX.
FIG. I.
IIII
II.
III.
V.
VI.
VII.
VIII.
IX.
X
XI
XII.
XIII.
XIIII.
XV.
XVI.
XVII.
XVIII.
XVII
XIX
XX
XXI
XXII
XXIII
XXIIII
XXV
XXVI
XXVII
XXVIII
XXIX
XXX
XX.

PLATE 21

FIGURE 1: Cranial nerves springing from the medulla oblongata.
FIGURE 2: Nerves of the cranium, with the cerebellum.
FIGURES 3–6: Further successive dissections of the cranial cavity.

TAB.XXI

FIG.I.

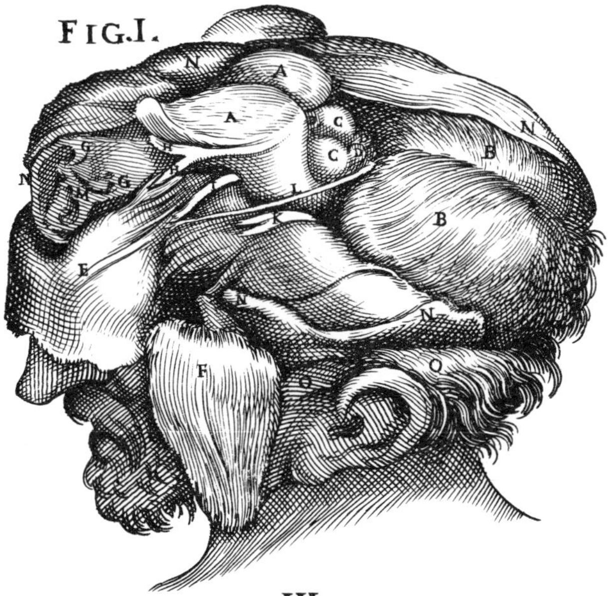

II

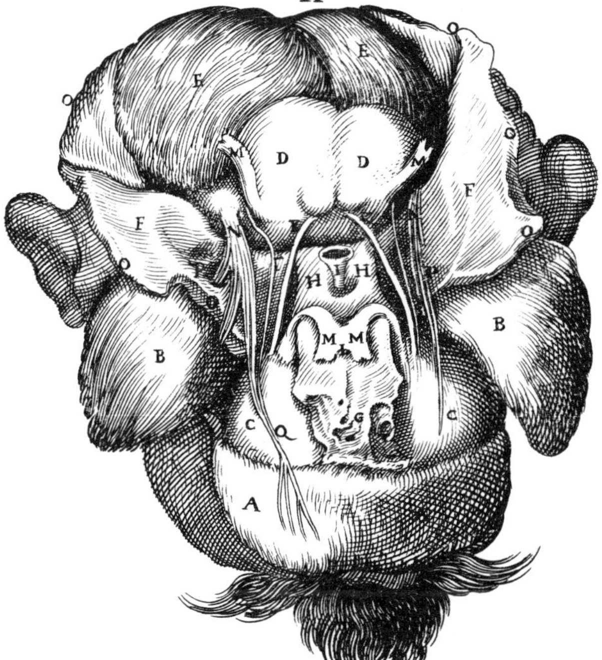

III

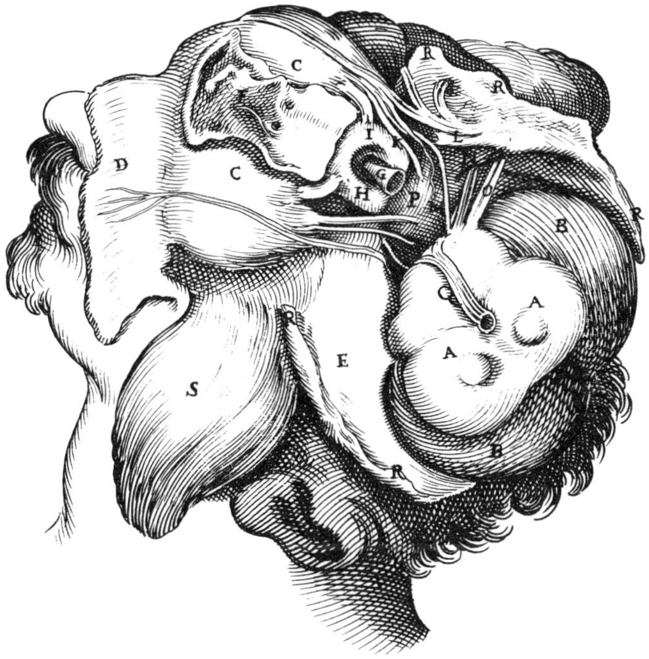

IIII

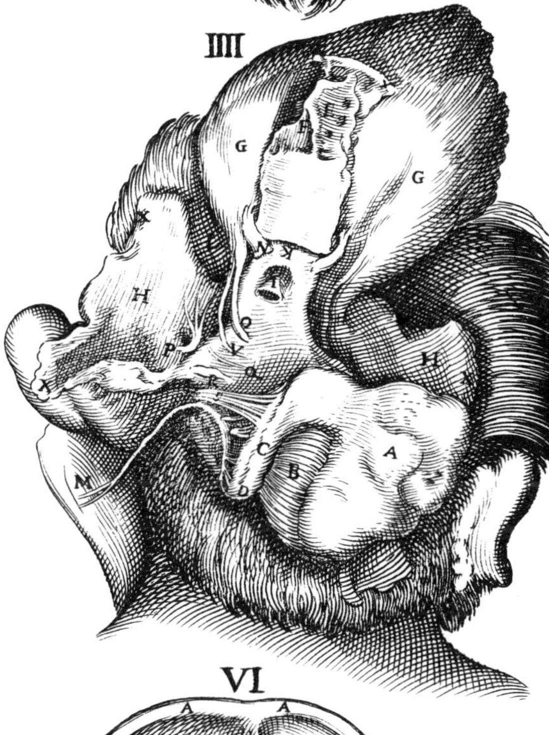

V

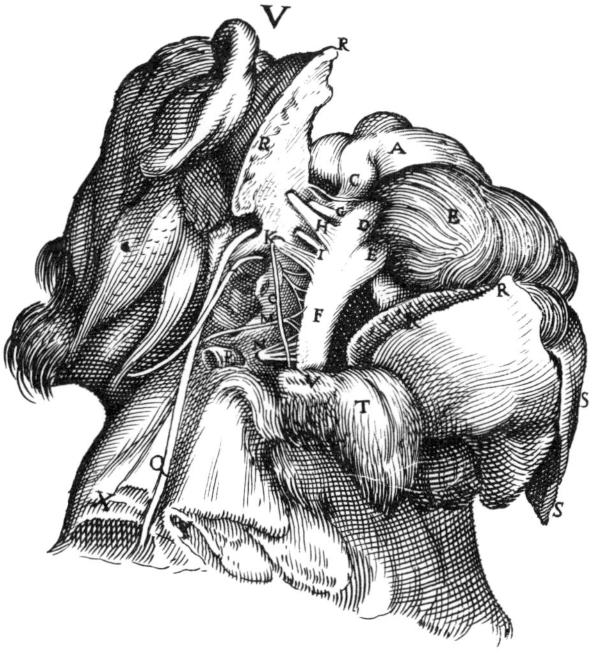

VI

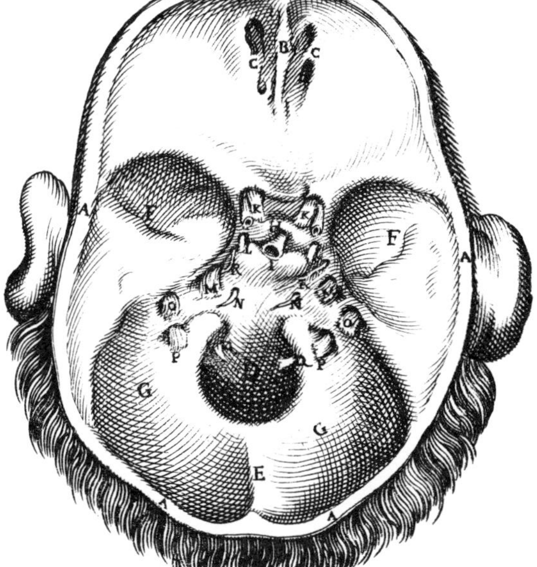

PLATE 22

FIGURE 1: Source of the optic nerve in the cerebrum.
FIGURES 2–18: Various views and dissections of the eye and associated muscles and nerves.

TAB. XXII.

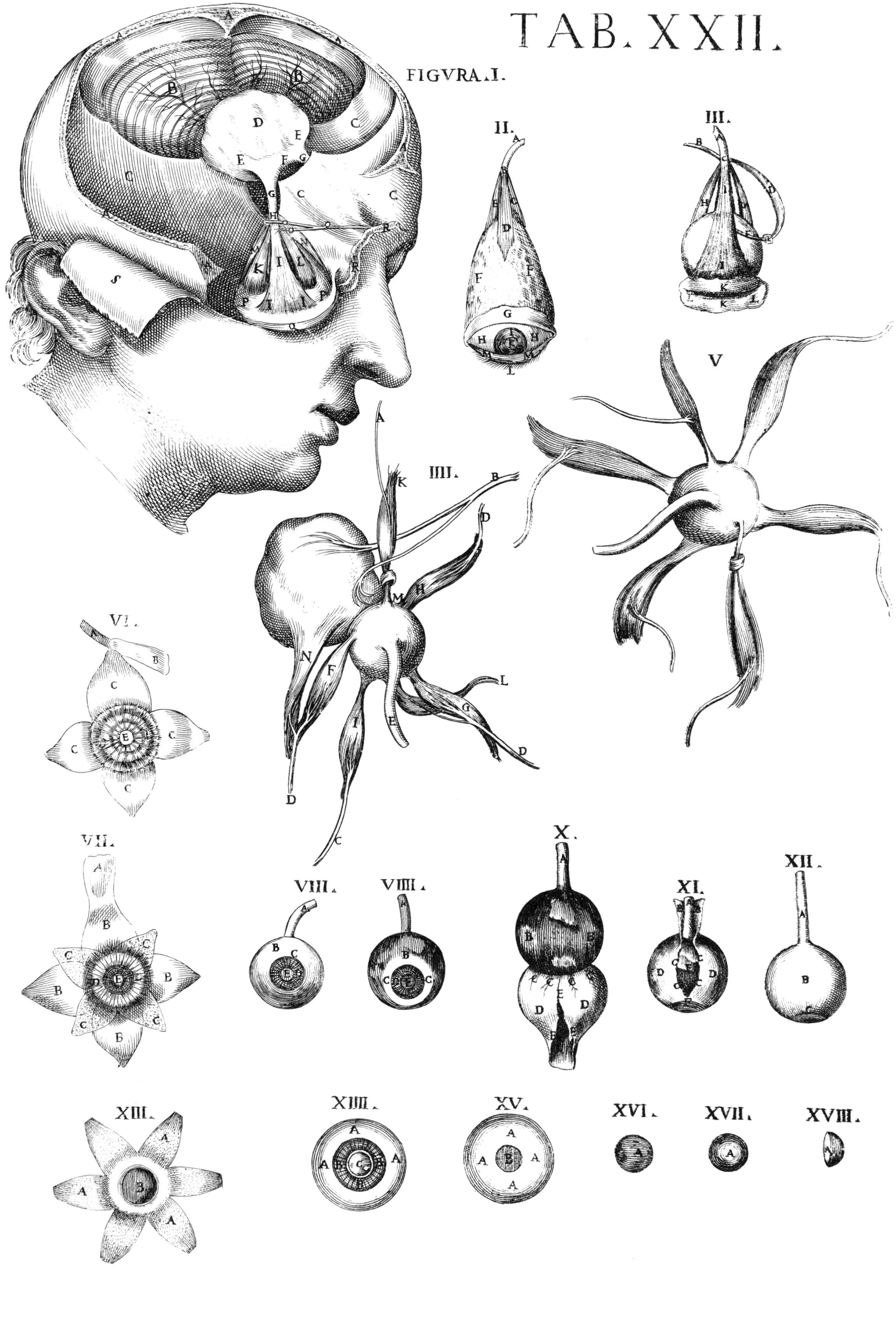

FIGVRA. I.
II.
III.
IIII.
V
VI.
VII.
VIII.
VIIII.
X.
XI.
XII.
XIII.
XIIII.
XV.
XVI.
XVII.
XVIII.

PLATE 23

Figure 1: External ear.
Figure 2: Muscles of the ear.
Figure 3: Temporal bone.
Figures 4–21: Other bones of the ear.

TAB. XXIII.

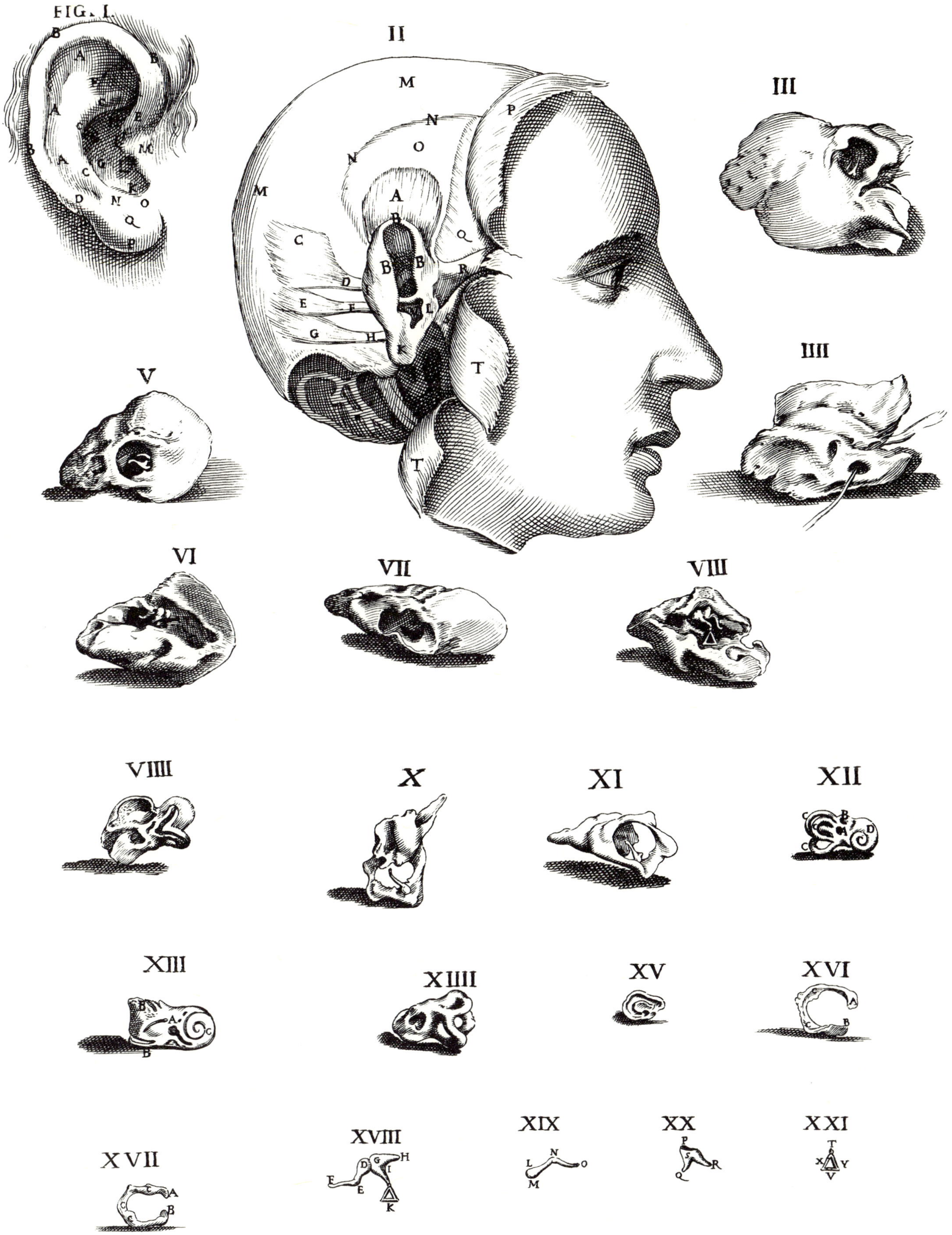
FIG. I.
II
III
IIII
V
VI
VII
VIII
VIIII
X
XI
XII
XIII
XIIII
XV
XVI
XVII
XVIII
XIX
XX
XXI

PLATE 24

FIGURE 1: Cutaneous veins.
FIGURE 2: Veins of the leg with (numbered) valves.
FIGURE 3: Veins of the arm with valves.
FIGURE 4: Dissection of an arm vein.

TAB. XXIIII

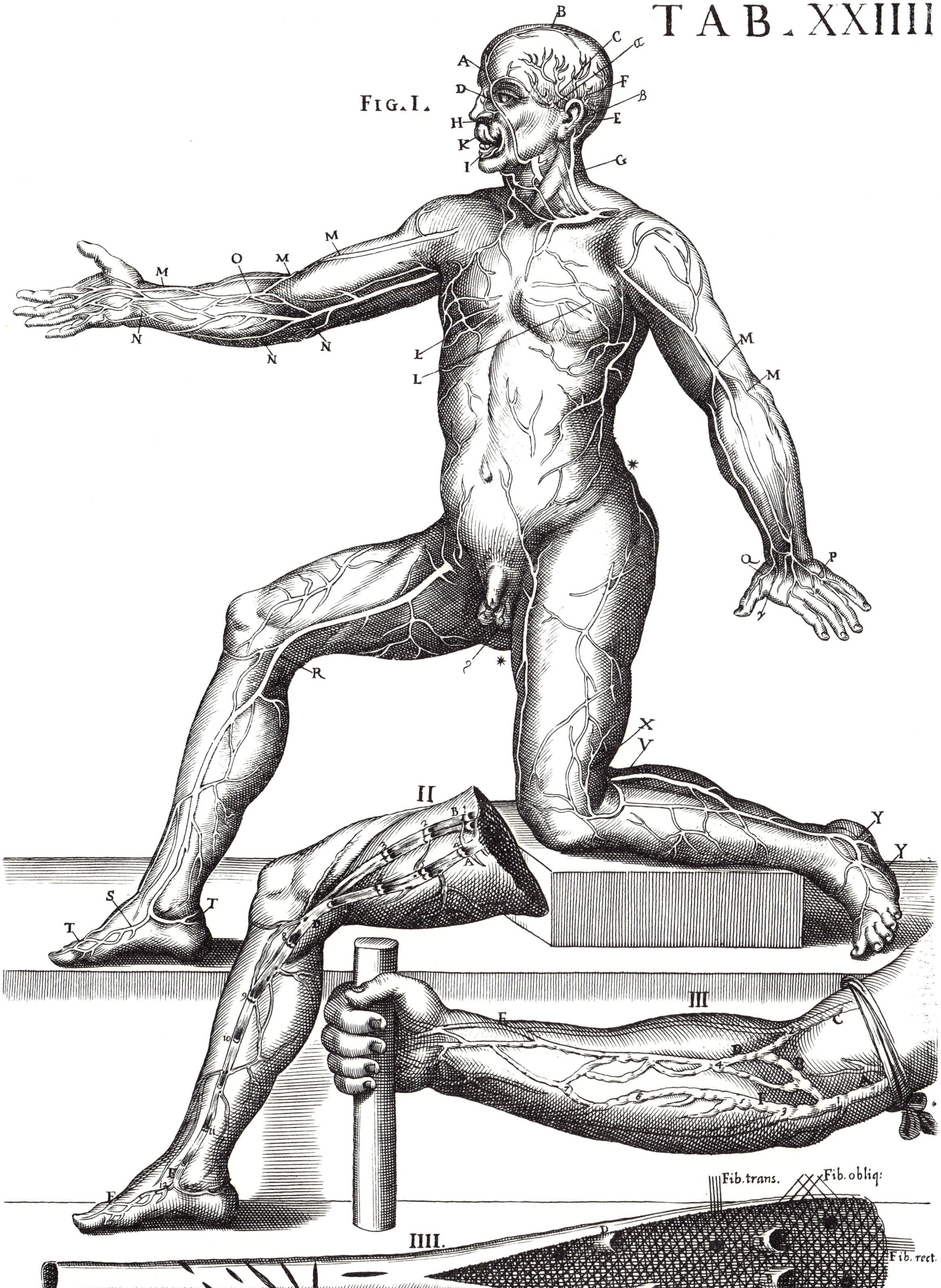

PLATE 25

FIGURES 1–5: Views of vertebrae.
FIGURE 6: Spinal column.
FIGURE 7: Spinal cord.

TAB. XXV

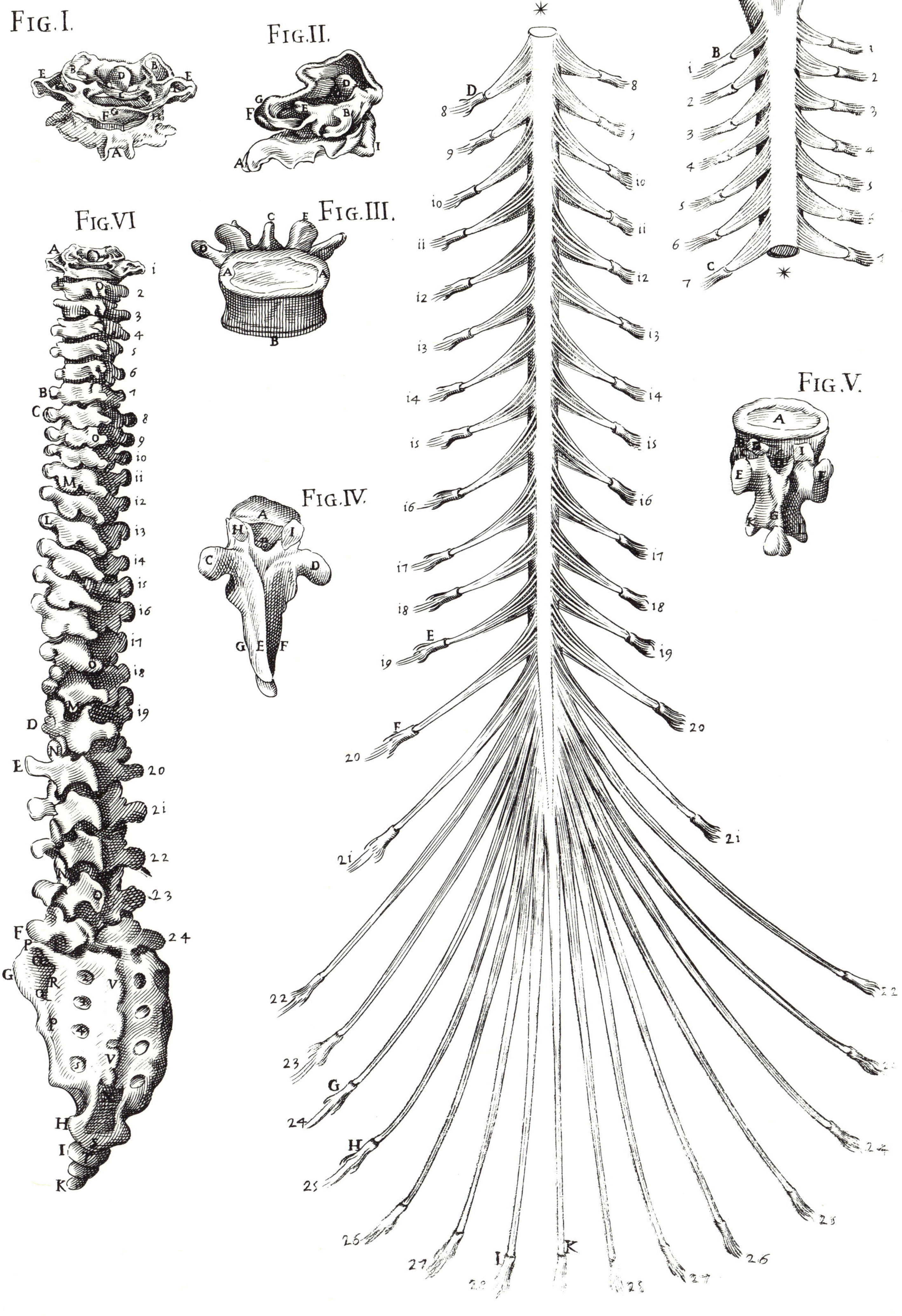

PLATE 26

Figures 1–3: Three views of the entire skeleton.

TAB XXVI

FIG. II. FIG. I. FIG. III.

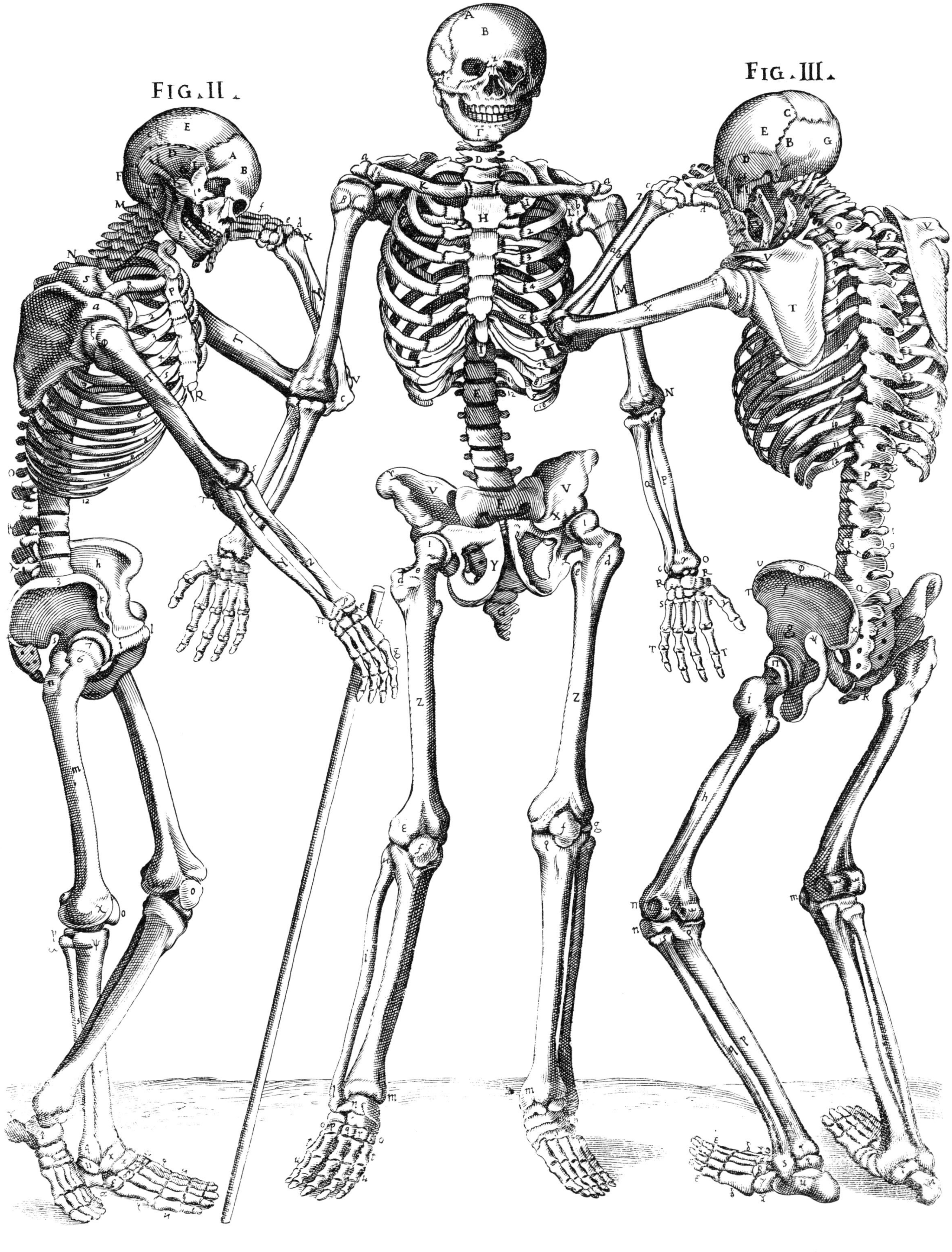

PLATE 27

FIGURE 1: Female urogenital system.
FIGURE 2: Closer view, with a fetus inside the uterus.

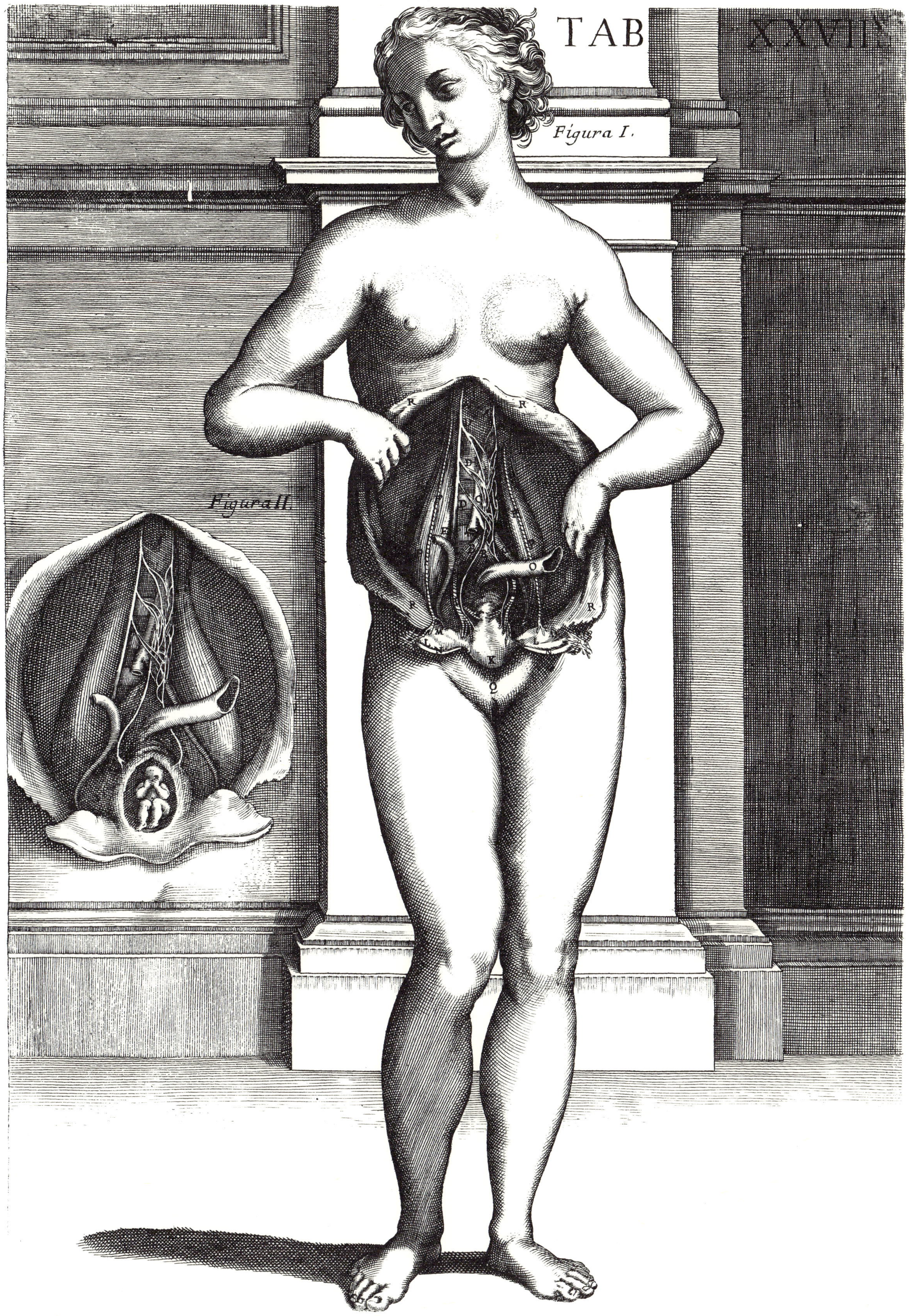
TAB XXVIII
Figura I.
Figura II.